OUT OF SIGHT

Also by Leslie and Sewell Stokes :

OSCAR WILDE: A PLAY IN THREE ACTS

OUT OF SIGHT

A Play About Prison

by

LESLIE AND SEWELL STOKES

London

MARTIN SECKER & WARBURG LTD

22 *Essex Street Strand*

1937

MADE IN GREAT BRITAIN

PRINTED BY THE LONDON AND NORWICH PRESS, LIMITED
ST. GILES WORKS, NORWICH

FOR

"PETER"

(E. M. COLLETT)

CHARACTERS

THE GOVERNOR	
THE REV. JOHN SAUNDERS (*The Chaplain*)	
DEREK FLEMING (" TOFF ")	*Prisoners*
RICHARDSON (" BATS ")	*Prisoners*
SMITH (" DUKE ")	*Prisoners*
JAMES PORTER	*Prisoners*
BILL RUDGE	*Prisoners*
MR. FIELD	*Prison Officers*
MR. BATES	*Prison Officers*
MR. MORTON	*Prison Officers*
MARY FIELD	
LILY PORTER	
MABEL RUDGE	

"OUT OF SIGHT" was first presented in London at the Gate Theatre on March 4, 1937, with the following cast:

THE GOVERNOR	ROBERT RENDEL
THE REV. JOHN SAUNDERS	BRIAN OULTON
DEREK FLEMING	JOHN ROBINSON
RICHARDSON	HARRY HUTCHINSON
SMITH	ROY CAMBRIAN
PORTER	CHARLES LEFEAUX
RUDGE	FRANK FOSTER
FIELD	DOUGLAS BURBIDGE
BATES	GEOFFREY WEARING
MORTON	MICHAEL MORICE
MARY FIELD	VIVIENNE BENNETT
LILY PORTER	JILL FURSE
MABEL RUDGE	PHYLLIS MORRIS

Play directed by NORMAN MARSHALL

SCENES

ACT I

SCENE 1. *The Governor's Office.*

SCENE 2. *Reception Hall.*

SCENE 3. *The Cells.*

ACT II

SCENE 1. *Outside the Cells. Eighteen months later.*

SCENE 2. *Mr. Field's Parlour.*

SCENE 3. *A Visiting Room.*

SCENE 4. *Outside the Cells.*

ACT III

SCENE 1. *Mr. Field's Parlour.*

SCENE 2. *A Punishment Cell.*

SCENE 3. *The Governor's Office. Three and a half years later.*

The action of the play covers five years and takes place within the boundaries of one of His Majesty's Convict Prisons.

ACT I

Scene i

Scene: *The Governor's office late one winter afternoon.*

It is a comfortable room with one door and a large window barred on the outside. A fire is burning in the grate. The furniture comprises a flat desk, chairs, book-case, filing-cabinet, and carpet. When the curtain rises the stage is lit only by the flicker of the fire. Dimly is seen the figure of Duke, *holding steady a ladder on the top of which stands* Bats, *mending a light that hangs from the ceiling. The light flashes on only long enough for us to see that both are wearing the grey prison uniform. Each has a red armlet buttoned on one sleeve indicating that he is a trusted prisoner. Then all is darkness again.*

Duke: What's the matter with the blasted thing! Shall I have a try?

Bats: There's no need to be swearing. Foul language won't mend it any the sooner.

The light flashes on again, long enough this time for us to observe that Bats *is a thin man, old beyond his forty-five years, with the strangely vague look of one who lives almost entirely in a world of his own.* Duke, *on the other hand, though about the same age, is plumper than he would like to be. From the fact that his hair is plastered down with fat and his trousers creased, we gather that he is something of a dandy.* BATS'S *voice is naturally rough*; DUKE'S *is self-consciously refined, though scarcely refined enough to cover what is more than a trace of a Cockney accent. Once more the light fails.*

DUKE: It's gone again; God damn it!

BATS (*who is never anything but serious*): The Lord will not hold him guiltless that taketh His name in vain.

DUKE: When you've finished the Sermon on the Mount, perhaps you'll fix the light.

BATS: I'm doing me best. As I always try to do.

DUKE (*resignedly*): O.K. But be quick. I'm tired of holding on to this ladder.

The light flashes on, this time for good.

BATS: It's mended now. (*He starts carefully to descend.*)

DUKE (*helping him by the hand*): That's fine! Gently now, Bats. (*As* BATS *reaches the ground, the sound of a band playing a spirited fox-trot is heard through the window.* DUKE *continues to hold the other's hand*) It's the jolly old prison band, practising for next week's concert. May I, Miss Bats, have the pleasure of this dance?

BATS (*shaking him off, impatiently*): Can't you never stop playing the fool? (*With his head on one side he listens*) What kind of music d'you call that?

DUKE (*who has picked up a cushion, and is dancing round the room with it*): It's a new hot number. I've heard it on the wireless, over in the recreation room. We're getting quite up to date in this hole.

BATS (*nodding his head*): A hot number. It's well named. Satan's music, that's what it is.

DUKE (*interested in his dance*): Maybe you're right. All I can say is, Satan knows how to write a good tune.

BATS: When I first come here, there was no prison band. I'm not sure we weren't better off without it.

DUKE: You came here in the dark ages. There's been progress since then.

BATS: Progress, you call it! Not when they play them heathen tunes, it isn't. (*Hopefully*) Now, if they'd give us a nice hymn. . . .

Abruptly the music ceases. Annoyed, DUKE *comes to a standstill by the desk, then sits on it.*

DUKE: Always grumbling, you are. Now see what you've done. The musicians must have heard you, and taken offence!

BATS (*muttering to himself*): Hot music! That's what the world's come to. No decency anywhere. Not even here, in prison. . . . (*He starts to collect from the floor at his feet the tools with which he has been working*) Hot music. . . .

DUKE (*who has discovered a copy of the "Tatler" in a drawer of the desk, and is looking at the pictures*) I say! Here's a nice pair of legs. (*Reads*) "Lady Ursula Ashby enjoying the sun at Cannes." She is, too. Every bit of her. (*Peers more closely at picture, then holds it out to* BATS) Care to give your eyes a treat?

BATS: Must you always be poking your nose where it doesn't belong? Put that back now, and come along. We've finished this job. What will the Governor say, if he finds us still hanging about his room?

DUKE (*gazing at the paper again*): I expect he'll invite us to supper. Nice little shassy she's got, too. Just my type.

BATS (*who has crossed to the desk, and is peering over* DUKE'S *shoulder, accusingly*): She's a whore! That's what she is.

DUKE (*surprised*): Steady on. What's up?

BATS: The brazen creature. Uncovering herself, and smiling about it.

DUKE: You'll say it's wrong to smile next! (*seriously*) You chaps with life-sentences are all the same. Never see any good in anybody! Depressing, I call it.

BATS (*tapping the paper with his forefinger*): There's never any good in a woman of her sort. (*After a pause; bitterly*) There's precious little good in any woman, what I've seen of 'em.

DUKE (*laughing*): And that's a fat lot! I doubt if you've seen a real woman in the ten years you've been here. Not counting the old girls that turn up to give us a concert now and again. They're not women. (*Shudders at the thought*) The faces some of them have got! And the figures! It's my belief they're not human. Just manufactured by the Home Office. Guaranteed not to give men ideas.

BATS (*wearily*): When you've finished chattering, we'll get over to Reception. We'll be needed there soon. There's new prisoners coming in to-night.

DUKE: What's the hurry? (*Crosses to fire and warms his hands*) Makes a nice change being in here. It's seldom enough we get the chance to be inside a real room. Personal comfort has always meant a lot to me. (*Affectedly*) I'm oddly sensitive that way.

BATS: I found a sailor's life comfortable enough—once. Soft living never did nobody any good.

(*Changing the subject*) There'll be trouble if we're found here doing nothing. We'll be 'cased.'

DUKE (*brushing the possibility aside*): Of course we won't. (*Warming to the subject*) Talking of women . . .

BATS: It's you what's doing the talking.

DUKE: Well, you must admit I'm a bit of an authority on the subject.

BATS (*looking at him curiously*): Six times you was married, wasn't you? In a manner of speaking, that is.

DUKE (*with conceit*): Seven—counting my legal wife. Six times bigamously. (*Thoughtfully*) Women have been good to me.

BATS (*sarcastically*): I wonder why.

DUKE: Did I ever tell you what the *News of the World* said about me? They put it rather well, I thought. (*Closing his eyes he repeats from memory*) The adventures in matrimony that thrilled the court were those of William Smith, alias de Winton Gore-Brown, alias Anthony d'Arcy, 45, described as independent. Tall and good-looking, with clean-cut features, William Smith has for most of his adventurous life exercised an uncanny influence over women. This is largely because his prepossessing looks are allied to pleasant, cultivated speech and polished manners. (*Opening his eyes*) What do you think of that?

BATS (*seriously*): It's a wonder you're not ashamed to repeat the words. (*Beginning to lose control*) It's scum like you that makes women—even good women—turn against their men . . .

DUKE: Who are you calling scum?

BATS : That's what you are! And it's about time somebody told you.

DUKE (*sneeringly*) : And I suppose you think you're the right one to do it. (*Jeeringly*) A dirty murderer, that's what you are. I'd sooner be in for bigamy than *murder*. (*He avoids* BATS, *who threateningly chases him round the room*) Strangled your wife, and only escaped the hangman's rope because you'd found her in bed with another man. And who'd blame her, with you for a husband! Dirty murderer! Dirty murderer!

BATS (*suddenly catching hold of his tormentor*) : As God's my witness, I'll . . .

The men are interrupted by the quick entrance of FIELD, *a senior officer of the prison. He seizes hold of them, as if they were two children, whose heads he intends banging together. He looks from one to the other, in a not unfatherly manner. Immediately both men appear pathetically intimidated.*

FIELD (*sharply*) : Now what's all this about? Let's have it. (*As neither answers*) D'you both want to be put on report for scrapping? (*To* BATS) I'm surprised at *you*, Bats.

BATS (*pathetically*) : He shouldn't have called me a murderer.

FIELD : So that's the trouble! (*Releasing them*) Now, Bats, you be off with that ladder, and I'll see you over at Reception in a minute or two. (*To* DUKE, *who is moving towards the door*) Hold on there, Duke, I've got something to say to you.

Muttering to himself, BATS *goes out carrying the ladder. When he has gone,* FIELD *turns to* DUKE.

FIELD : I thought you'd more sense, man, than to go

teasing old Bats. You know as well as I do that to him the word murderer is like a red rag to a bull.

DUKE (*sulkily*) : He started it.

FIELD : I don't give a damn who started it. You've been here long enough to know that Lifers have to be treated carefully. Every one of them's a bit touched, and liable to go off the deep end at any moment. You'd be that way yourself after ten years in this place.

DUKE (*ashamed of himself*) : I'm sorry, sir.

FIELD : So you ought to be. Come along now, we've no time to waste.

DUKE *is about to follow* FIELD *out, when the door is opened, and the* REV. JOHN SAUNDERS *is ushered in by* MORTON.

MORTON (*to* SAUNDERS) : This way, sir. I'll tell the Governor you're here.

SAUNDERS : Thanks.

FIELD, *having saluted smartly, goes out, followed by* DUKE, *who stares curiously at* SAUNDERS. *The prison band strikes up again.*

(*smiling*) Music! I didn't expect to find that here.

MORTON : No, sir? It's the men practising for next week's concert. Some of them aren't bad musicians, sir.

SAUNDERS : They sound quite professional.

MORTON : Yes, sir. The Governor won't keep you long, sir.

MORTON *salutes and goes out. Left alone,* SAUNDERS *goes to the window and looks out. He is a young man, and wears a clerical collar. He beats time to the music with his foot. Then he comes back into the room and takes in its details with interest. He picks up a book from the desk, and glances through it. A page holds his attention, so that he does not notice* BATS, *who comes slowly into the room, and stands staring at the stranger. As the music ceases abruptly,* SAUNDERS *looks up, and for a few seconds the two men face each other in silence.*

BATS (*who cannot take his eyes from the clerical collar*): If you'll excuse me, sir. I came to fetch the tools I left here.

SAUNDERS: Right you are. Go ahead. (*He pretends to return to his book, but really is watching* BATS, *who is the first prisoner he has seen.* BATS, *on his knees, is gathering up the tools from the floor, but cannot resist turning his head to have another look at* SAUNDERS. *Their eyes meet again. Pleasantly*) What's your name?

BATS: Richardson, sir. They call me Bats, here. Think I'm not quite right in the head. But I am, of course. Too right, for some of them. (*After a pause*) Beg pardon, sir, but are you the new sky-pilot? Chaplain, I mean, sir.

SAUNDERS (*trying to be as natural as possible*): Yes, I'm to be your new chaplain. (*Cheerfully*) I hope we're going to be friends.

BATS (*passionately*): Oh, I do hope so, sir. (*Sadly*) There's times when I feel the need of a friend.

SAUNDERS: You know, I'm rather hoping to make a lot of friends while I'm here.

BATS (*Reflectively*): I expect you'll find them a queer crowd.

SAUNDERS: Well, this is my first experience of a prison, but I'm looking forward to the work.

BATS: All sorts, you'll come across here. (*Changing his tone to one of recitation*) For from within, out of the heart of men, proceed evil thoughts, adulteries, fornications, murders, thefts, blasphemy, foolishness. All these things come from within and defile a man.

SAUNDERS (*embarrassed, but trying to disguise the fact*): I didn't come here expecting to find saints, you know.

BATS: You'll not find them. (*After a pause*) Why do you think I was sent here? (*As* SAUNDERS *shakes his head and smiles good-humouredly*) I murdered me wife. (*Looking at his hands*) With them two hands I strangled the rotten life out of her. (*As* SAUNDERS *says nothing*) She was a bad woman. A proper harlot. Better dead. Only I was wrong to kill her. I see that now. I should have left it to God to do that.

SAUNDERS (*bewildered*): To God?

BATS: It was His work to punish her—not mine. And it's He who's punishing me now, for taking too much upon myself. I'm not complaining. God's always just. And when me sentence is over, and I leave prison, I'm going to be a preacher. I'll never stop telling people how God saved me. Everywhere I'll preach the Gospel to sinners; telling them how I was saved, when I thought me last hour had come . . .

Just before BATS *has finished, the* GOVERNOR *strides into the room. He is a middle-aged man, pleasant, quick in his movements, and after the somewhat grim atmosphere that has been created by* BATS, *his presence comes as a relief. His manner is always breezy.*

GOVERNOR (*cutting in on* BATS): What are you doing here?

BATS (*humbly*): I came to mend the light, sir, and . .

GOVERNOR (*looking at light*): Is it mended?

BATS: Yes, sir. It's . . .

GOVERNOR: Get along then, there's a good fellow.

BATS (*carrying out the tools he has collected*): Yes, sir.

SAUNDERS *stares after the retreating figure of* BATS *rather as if he were watching a ghost disappear. The* GOVERNOR *pats him on the back.*

GOVERNOR: How are you, John?

SAUNDERS (*partly recovering himself*): Oh, all right, sir—thanks.

GOVERNOR (*smiling, and in a matter-of-fact voice*): Old Bats been telling you the story of his life?

SAUNDERS: He said he'd murdered his wife.

GOVERNOR: That's right. Came home on leave, found her carrying on with another man, and strangled her. Got his reprieve at the last moment. (*Dismissing the subject from his mind*) Well, John, full of enthusiasm for your new work? Determined to relieve the unhappy lot of the convict. (*Smiling*) Well, you can't say I didn't do my best to dissuade you from coming. Sit down.

The GOVERNOR *sits at his desk, and* SAUNDERS *takes the armchair.*

(*Looking at* SAUNDERS) You know, John, you mustn't expect to find things very easy here.

SAUNDERS (*enthusiastically*): I don't, sir. I'm not afraid of hard work.

GOVERNOR: That's not quite what I mean. (*After a pause*) Yours isn't a job I'd wish on anybody. I told your father that, when he came to see me about you. But he said you'd quite made up your mind. (*With a gesture of the hands*) And so . . .

SAUNDERS: This kind of work appeals to me. I've always wanted to do it.

GOVERNOR: That's because you know absolutely nothing about it. Nobody can be expected to, until they come here, and see for themselves how things are. Frankly, John, I wish you hadn't come.

SAUNDERS: Why do you wish that, sir?

The GOVERNOR *wanders over to the fireplace. Then he turns round.*

GOVERNOR: I'm going to speak to you pretty candidly, John; as I dare say a governor has no right to speak to his new chaplain. As man to man, if you like. I've known your father all my life, and you since you were a small boy. (*He pauses, before continuing*) You come here, not without experience in an East End parish, it's true; but with no knowledge whatever of what prison conditions are really like. Well, I'll tell you what they're like. (*With conviction*) They're pretty hopeless.

SAUNDERS (*if anything, encouraged*): Then perhaps, sir, in my small way, I can do something to better those conditions?

GOVERNOR: You think so? (*Laughs*) I only wish I could think so too. (*He takes a book from the desk, and finds in it the place he wants*) Listen to this. (*He reads*) "Prison treatment should have as its primary and concurrent objects deterrence and reformation; effectually designed to maintain, stimulate, or awaken the higher susceptibilities of prisoners; and turn them out of prison better men and women, both physically and morally, than when they came in." Are you listening?

SAUNDERS: Yes, sir; I'm listening.

GOVERNOR (*continues reading*): "I regard as unfavourable to a prisoner's reformation the crushing of self-respect, the starving of all moral instincts he may possess, the continual association with none but criminals, the absence of all opportunity of doing or receiving a kindness, the forced labour and the denial of liberty. I believe the true mode of reforming a man or restoring him to society is exactly in the opposite direction of all these. (*With emphasis*) But of course the unfavourable features I have mentioned are inseparable from prison life." (*He throws the book down on the desk*) And that was written by a prison commissioner, who knew what he was talking about.

SAUNDERS (*rising from his chair*): He takes a pretty gloomy view of things, doesn't he?

GOVERNOR: It's not easy to take any other view.

SAUNDERS (*hesitatingly*): But, sir . . .

GOVERNOR: Well?

SAUNDERS: You've spent your life in the Prison Service. And I don't imagine it's been wasted.

GOVERNOR (*reflectively*): I like to think it hasn't. But I'm not sure. I dare say there are worse governors than I am. Possibly better ones. All of us try to do our best. But I'm afraid an out-of-date system makes our efforts rather useless. The most we can do is to try and be human—even if it is against the regulations.

SAUNDERS: I see . . .

GOVERNOR (*sits at desk again, and takes up a sheet of paper*): Here are the names of three men coming in to-night. Fleming—for fraudulent conversion. Rudge—he's an old lag—for theft. Porter—for some crime against the Official Secrets Act. Each of them has got a five-year sentence. And what good d'you suppose it's going to do them ? No damned good at all.

SAUNDERS : I suppose criminals must be reformed ?

GOVERNOR : Of course they must. But they aren't. That's the whole point. What's going to happen to these men in the next five years ? They're going to lose their liberty. They're going to live under lock and key, behind a twenty foot wall, in a bleak atmosphere of discomfort and disgrace, under rigid discipline and constant supervision. They won't have even the smallest luxury or comfort ; they'll be subject to forced labour ; they'll be cut off from family and friends, from the society of the other sex, and from all natural human intercourse. (*Contemptuously*) Is that going to reform them ?

SAUNDERS : It does all sound pretty grim. But what would you do about it ?

GOVERNOR : There are plenty of things I'd like to do, if I had the authority. I'd begin by treating the men as if they were natural human beings. I'd begin by trying to encourage their self-respect, instead of deliberately crushing it.

There is a knock at the door.

Come in !

FIELD *enters and salutes.*

What is it, Field ?

FIELD (*mechanically*) : A man over in C Hall has just tried to commit suicide by putting his head in a bucket of water, sir.

GOVERNOR : Is the doctor with him ?

FIELD : Yes, sir. He's bringing him round now, in the hospital.

GOVERNOR : All right, Field. I'll be over later.

FIELD *salutes, and goes.*

SAUNDERS (*who has been horrified by what he has heard*): Poor devil.

GOVERNOR: What? Oh, that. You'll soon get used to those little episodes. They're all in the day's work. Come along to the Reception, now, and we'll take a look at the new men.

As they go out, the band strikes up the fox-trot, and the curtain falls.

SCENE 2

SCENE: *The Reception Hall of the Prison. A wide corridor, at the back of which are seen the outsides of three cubicles, each with a small swing-door well raised above the floor. On the audience's left is a desk at which* FIELD *is writing when the curtain rises; and directly opposite this, on the right, is a long, low bench. Back centre stands a pair of scales with a device attached to it for measuring a man's height and the width of his outstretched arms.*

After the entrance of the three new prisoners, this scene is played quickly by the entire cast, as it is necessary to gain an atmosphere of bustle and hurry. But it opens slowly.

From the left enter BATS *and* DUKE, *each carrying in his arms a pile of prison uniforms, including shoes, shirts, jackets, waistcoats, trousers, socks, braces, ties, and three large white canvas bags. These, with every evidence of relief, they dump in the centre of the stage.*

DUKE : I'm sorry, Bats, about what happened just now. I didn't mean any harm.

BATS : We'll say no more about it.

DUKE (*to* FIELD) : The Receptions will be here any minute now, sir. The van's just come in.

FIELD (*without looking up from his writing*) : Good. I'm ready for them.

Exit BATS *and* DUKE. *Enter from the right, whistling,* BATES, *a young-looking officer. He stops by the desk and looks over* FIELD'S *shoulder.*

BATES : Any of the new prisoners interesting ?

FIELD : Depends what you call interesting.

BATES : Well, anyone notorious ?

FIELD : I shouldn't bother to get your autograph book, if I was you.

BATES : We do get a tame lot 'ere. Since I've been in the Service, and that'll be a year come Christmas, I haven't set eyes on one new murderer. (*After a pause*) I'm beginning to think that life in the army was more exciting.

FIELD : Why didn't you stay in the army ?

BATES : Too much like work for me. And you're treated worse than dirt. Might as well be a convict, as be a private in the Guards.

FIELD : So you thought you'd try the Prison Service, and boss other people, instead of being bossed yourself ? I know you youngsters who come here out of the army. You're all the same. Well, take a bit of advice from one who's been in this job a long time : keep the men as sweet as you can. They're easier to handle that way.

BATES : Strikes me you're a sight too easy with them sometimes.

FIELD : It does, does it ? Let me tell you something. I get more work out of my men than any other officer in this prison. Why ? Because I try to treat them like human beings. And you won't go far wrong if you do the same. Ours isn't a pleasant job at the best of times. But we needn't overdo the heavy stuff.

Enter DUKE, *left, carrying a pile of prayer and library books, which he places on the end of the bench nearest the audience.*

DUKE (*to* BATES, *as he goes out again*) : Please, sir, who won the match this afternoon ?

BATES : How should I know ?

FIELDS (*without looking up from his writing*) : Chelsea won. Two-nil.

DUKE : Thank you, sir. (*Exit.*)

BATES *and* FIELD *look at each other significantly.*

BATES : I'm off at eight to-night. Think I'll go to the pictures. Makes a bit of a change.

FIELD (*only mildly interested*) : What's the film at the local ?

BATES : " Murder In The Big House."

FIELD (*laughing*) : That *will* make a nice change.

BATES : You can laugh. You're a married man, with a nice missis to go home to. Now if I was married to a pretty girl like Mrs. Field . . . She's all right.

FIELD : Glad you like her.

BATES : You're a lucky man.

FIELD : D'you know, I think I am.

BATES (*as sound of marching is heard*) : Here come the Receptions.

FIELD *stands up.* FLEMING, PORTER, *and* RUDGE *are marched in by* MORTON.

MORTON (*to prisoners*): Halt! (*Pointing to bench*) Sit yerselves down there, and don't make a row. (*To* FIELD) Three receptions—all correct, sir! (*Hands him a paper.*)

FIELD (*taking paper*): Right, sir.

Exit MORTON. FIELD *resumes his seat, and takes a good look at the three prisoners, who are wearing hats and overcoats.* FLEMING, *a good-looking man of thirty, is obviously a gentleman and feeling his position.* RUDGE, *about forty-five, is a member of the criminal class, and doesn't care who knows it.* PORTER *might be any little city clerk, and his age is about forty. All the men look miserable.*

Now just answer to your names, will you? Derek Fleming?

FLEMING: Yes.

FIELD: James Porter?

PORTER: Here, sir.

FIELD: William Rudge? (*There is no answer, as* RUDGE *is intent on picking his nails*) William Rudge!

RUDGE (*grudgingly*): Here . . .

FIELD: Here—what?

RUDGE (*sarcastically*): Here—sir. (*To* PORTER) Fancy having to call that sir!

FIELD: I heard you.

RUDGE: What about it?

FIELD (*quietly*): I should have thought you'd been in prison enough times to know the rules, and how to address an officer properly.

RUDGE: The blasted rules is always changing. When I first come to one of these places you was called warders. Now it's officers. But the men call you 'screws,' and always will.

FIELD (*ignoring him, to the others*) : Now I want you to come up here in turn, and answer the questions I put to you. Fleming ?

BATES (*to* FLEMING, *pointing to front of desk*) : Stand up there !

FLEMING *does as he is told.*

FIELD : Name in full ?

FLEMING : Derek Fleming.

FIELD (*having entered the answer in his book*) : Profession ?

FLEMING : I was a solicitor.

FIELD : Domicile ?

FLEMING : Reading.

FIELD : Colour of hair ?

FLEMING (*slowly*) : Light brown.

FIELD : Colour of eyes ?

FLEMING : I'm not sure, sir.

FIELD (*looking at them*) : I'll put grey. Religion ?

FLEMING : Catholic.

FIELD : Special peculiarities ?

FLEMING (*smiling*) : I don't know that I've got any.

FIELD : All right. Next !

BATES (*to* PORTER) : Come on, look sharp ! (*To* FLEMING, *indicating the first cubicle*) In there, and get yer things off. And when you're ready come out to be measured.

PORTER *and* FLEMING *obey.* DUKE *enters from left, carrying a pile of sheets and blankets which he deposits on the bench by the books. He is recognised by* RUDGE, *who at once claims him as a former prison acquaintance. Their dialogue is heard above the ex-*

change of questions and answers between FIELD *and* PORTER, *who now speak in undertones.*

RUDGE: Well, if it ain't the Duke! Wotcher me old cock sparrow! 'Ow many women is yer married to now?

DUKE (*on his dignity*): I don't recollect having met you before.

RUDGE: Come orf it! You and me did a stretch together at Birmingham. It's no use pretending you don't remember Bill Rudge. I don't suppose you ever knew who yer father was. But you do know me.

DUKE (*embarrassed*): Your face does seem familiar, I must admit.

RUDGE: Familiar me foot! You always did like to think yourself 'igh and mighty. There's a real toff come in with me to-night. (*Nods towards cubicle*) Fleming's the name. In for embezzlement. Been to Oxford and Cambridge and all them places. You don't stand an earthly with him 'ere. So you may as well come off yer perch, see? What's the grub like in this dump?

DUKE: Bloody awful!

RUDGE: Thought about as much. I know me poor stomach won't stand for it. (*Patting it*) It's getting a bit particular these days.

PORTER *is now shown into the second cubicle by* BATES.

FIELD: Rudge?

RUDGE (*to* DUKE): I shouldn't be here at all by rights. Just bleedin' bad luck. I . . .

FIELD (*shouting*): Rudge!

RUDGE (*to* FIELD): Was you calling *me*?

FIELD: No—Mussolini. But you'll do.

RUDGE *goes over to the desk. At the same time* BATS *enters from the left with a ledger and pencil, and crosses to the scales. As he reaches them* FLEMING *comes out of his cubicle naked except for a brown blanket tied round his middle.* BATES *takes him over to the scales, where he is weighed and measured,* BATES *calling out the figures, and* BATS *entering them in the ledger. This goes on simultaneously with the following dialogue.*

FIELD: Name in full?

RUDGE: William Algernon Rudge.

FIELD: Algernon?

RUDGE: You heard.

FIELD: Profession?

RUDGE: Independent.

FIELD: Domicile?

RUDGE: London.

FIELD: Colour of hair?

RUDGE (*sarcastically sweet*): What do *you* think?

FIELD (*writing*): Mouse. Colour of eyes?

RUDGE (*effeminately*): Violet.

FIELD: Religion?

RUDGE: None.

FIELD (*writing*): Church of England. Special peculiarities?

RUDGE: A mole on me back-side. Like to see it?

PORTER *comes from his cubicle, and changes places with* FLEMING *on the scales.* DUKE, *who has been sorting the pile of uniforms in the centre of the stage, then takes charge of him, being most affable.*

DUKE (*to* FLEMING, *pointing to cubicle*): Your bath's waiting through there. No bath salts, I'm afraid. I miss them so, don't you?

FLEMING (*smiling*) : I dare say I'll manage all right without them. (*He goes through the cubicle.*)

DUKE : I'll do my best to pick you a nice suit. The cut, of course, is frightful.

FLEMING (*as he goes through*) : Thanks very much.

PORTER'S *measurements are now being taken, simultaneously with the following dialogue, and during this* DUKE *is selecting garments one by one from the pile and flinging them into each of the three cubicles.*

FIELD (*looking up from the entries he has been making in his ledger*) : You and I will be seeing something of each other during the months to come, Rudge.

RUDGE : Won't that be nice, now ?

FIELD : We can work together—or against one another. I'd rather we worked together.

RUDGE : He's fallen for me !

FIELD : If your conduct's bad, I can get you punished.

RUDGE : But what you can't do, is to get me the sack !

FIELD : It's men like you, Rudge, who make prison life more difficult than it is already.

RUDGE : Have you ever considered that if it wasn't for the likes of me, the likes of you would be out of a job ? With no convicts there wouldn't be no warders. Oh, I beg your pardon—no *officers*.

FIELD : There are other jobs.

RUDGE : Not cushy ones, like yours. Where else would you get three pound a week, and yer house rent free, just for shouting ' Stop that talking ! ' and ' Close them doors ! ' Yours is a fine job. For men without brains.

FIELD (*who never loses his patience*) : Go along and get measured.

RUDGE *goes into his cubicle.* PORTER *goes to his bath. Enter* MORTON *from the right.*

MORTON : Governor's on his way. Bringing the new chaplain round. They'll be here in a minute.

At this information FIELD *and* BATES *straighten their peaked caps, and do up the top button of their tunics.* DUKE *straightens his tie, and quickens his movements.*

BATES : What's he like ?

MORTON : Who ? The new chaplain ? Not so dusty. Bit on the young side.

BATES : Well, the last one was too old. He 'adn't got no influence with the men. The chapel was empty most times.

MORTON : That's not surprising, seeing as he was always telling the men they was miserable sinners. I reckon it's bad taste to keep telling anyone he's a sinner.

BATES : It's damned rude, anyway.

BATS (*who has listened to every word*) : In the sight of the Lord we're all miserable sinners.

MORTON : Now we've started him off !

BATES (*kindly*) : Put a sock in it, Bats.

MORTON (*looking left ; in a whisper*) : Here comes the Governor.

As the GOVERNOR *and* SAUNDERS *enter all three officers stand to attention and salute.*

FIELD : All correct, sir. Two—and three away.

GOVERNOR (*taking paper from* FIELD) : Are these to-night's receptions ? (*He compares it with the list in his hand.*)

FIELD : Yes, sir.

GOVERNOR: Right. (*Hands paper back to* FIELD. *To* SAUNDERS): The new new arrivals—' receptions ' we call them—come in here first before being passed into the prison proper. I have to see each man in the morning. But sometimes I have a word with them at once. You might like to do the same.

SAUNDERS (*who has been looking round*): Thanks, I should.

FLEMING *comes out of his cubicle dressed in his prison uniform.*

DUKE (*Putting him wise, whispers*): The Governor. (*He hands* FLEMING *a canvas bag and motions him to hold it open, while into it he throws sheets, books, etc.*)

PORTER *comes out of his cubicle, wearing a uniform absurdly too large for him. He looks a most pathetic figure. He is almost dazed with grief.*

GOVERNOR (*addressing him*): Are you Porter?

PORTER *does not seem to hear.*

FIELD: The Governor's speaking to you!

PORTER (*to* GOVERNOR): I beg pardon, sir.

GOVERNOR (*friendly*): I'll have a word with you presently, Porter. Perhaps there's something you want to ask me?

PORTER: Thank you, sir.

FLEMING, *his canvas bag filled, sits on the bench.* PORTER, *helped by* DUKE, *gets his bag filled, and joins* FLEMING. *During this action* RUDGE, *bursting out of a uniform that ought to have been given to* PORTER, *comes out of his cubicle.*

RUDGE (*to the world at large*): Take a look at this, will you? (*To* DUKE) My tailor wouldn't arf be wild if he saw me. What are you going to do about it, that's what I want to know? I can stand up, but I'm bloody sure I can't sit down.

Suddenly he sees the GOVERNOR, *and stops.*

GOVERNOR: It's not a good fit, is it? (*To* FIELD) Get this man's kit changed in the morning.

FIELD: Yes, sir.

GOVERNOR (*to* RUDGE): I know your face, don't I?

RUDGE (*recognition dawning*): We was together at Rugby, sir! I did me first stretch there.

GOVERNOR: That's right. I was a deputy-governor in those days.

RUDGE: I'm glad you're here, sir; if you don't mind me saying so. You always treated us fair.

GOVERNOR: Thank you, Rudge. (*To* SAUNDERS) We'll get along to the hospital now, and you can see any of the men you want to later.

SAUNDERS: Right you are, sir.

As the GOVERNOR *and* SAUNDERS *go out the officers salute, after which the tension their entrance has caused relaxes.*

RUDGE (*getting his bag filled*): He's one of the best—and I know what I'm talking about.

BATES: You'll know what a punishment cell's like if you don't keep that trap of yours shut.

RUDGE: A real sweet nature you've got, 'aven't you?

BATES: You'll soon find out. Get on to the bench now.

RUDGE (*under his breath*): His mother must have been fond of kids to let him live.

With great difficulty, for his trousers are tight, RUDGE *sits down.*

FIELD (*addressing the men*) : Fall in now.

MORTON (*pointing*) : Down 'ere !

The prisoners obey, throwing their bags over their shoulders.

RUDGE : What an up and down life !

MORTON : Quick march !

The prisoners tramp out, followed by MORTON. BATS *and* DUKE *start clearing up.*

BATES (*to* FIELD, *as he looks after the retreating men*) : Well—what's your opinion of that little lot ?

FIELD : Can't help feeling sorry for the two that are in for the first time. They always get my sympathy.

BATES : Save your sympathy. I should. Being in here will teach 'em a lesson.

FIELD : Maybe.

CURTAIN

SCENE 3

THE CELLS : *This scene is twice divided by a black-out, which creates the illusion that we are taken to each of three cells, but the set is actually the same.*

The cell, thirteen feet broad by seven deep, has a rounded ceiling. The floor is of wood. The window is high up in the middle of the wall on the audience's left. In the middle of the opposite wall is the door, which opens inwards. Leaning against the centre of the back wall is a bed-board with mattress behind it. In the corner by the window is a quarter-circular, wooden, double shelf, on which are a slate, Bible and library books, tooth-

brush, and soap. The light is a bulb fixed above the door. There is a ventilator under the window, and another over the door. A chamber-pot with lid is under the window, and in the back wall are about three hooks, on one of which hang cards with printed matter on them.

When the curtain rises FLEMING *is sitting on his deal chair, staring blankly at the floor. Raising his head he notices the cards hanging on the wall, reaches for one, and starts to read it, murmuring the words.*

FLEMING (*slowly*): Savoury pie; sea pie; treacle-duff; pork and beans. . . . Each men is allowed eight ounces of bread . . .

The sound of a key turning in the double-lock is heard, and the door is flung open, revealing MORTON, *and directly behind him* DUKE. FLEMING *gets to his feet.*

MORTON: This man will show you how to put your cell in order. (*To* DUKE) And don't take all night about it! (*Exit, leaving door half open.*)

DUKE (*nodding after him*): So polite, aren't they? (*Seeing the card in* FLEMING's *hand*) Ah! You've been studying the menu.

FLEMING: It doesn't look too bad to me.

DUKE: It *looks* all right—in print. But it ought never to be translated into actual food. Not the same thing at all. You'll see. You'll see lots of things while you're here.

FLEMING: I expect I shall.

DUKE (*pointing to a bell-push by the door*): That bell, for example. When you push it, an indicator outside shows the officer on duty which cell is ringing. You might want to ring it if you felt ill in the night.

FLEMING: Rather a good idea.

DUKE: Quite a good idea. Only no officer has ever been known to answer a bell yet. (*Suddenly seeing* FLEMING's *shoes*) You mustn't wear your shoes in the cell. Let's find your slippers. (*He empties the contents of the canvas bag on to the floor*) Here they are. (*Hands them to* FLEMING) You must always put your shoes outside the door at night. Like you would in a hotel. Only you don't get them cleaned here.

FLEMING *changes into his slippers.*

You may as well get undressed now, and I'll make up your bed for you. It'll soon be lights out.

FLEMING: Thank you very much.

DUKE: Don't mention it. A pleasure.

During the rest of the scene FLEMING *undresses to his shirt, and* DUKE *makes up the bed, and generally sets the cell in order.*

FLEMING: I suppose they don't give one pyjamas here?

DUKE: Good gracious no; they haven't even heard of them. We sleep in our shirts. *And* we're only allowed one bath a week. Which is more than some of the men care about. A common lot they are, on the whole.

FLEMING (*reflectively*): That accounts for it.

DUKE: For what?

FLEMING (*sniffing*): For the odour of carbolic and—humanity.

DUKE: You've got five years, haven't you?

FLEMING: Five years.

DUKE: That's a terrible sentence for a first offence.

FLEMING: The judge seemed to think mine was a terrible crime. I expect it was. Only, you know, one's own crime never appears to be as bad as anybody else's. They say that to know all is to forgive all—and one forgives oneself so easily.

DUKE: I can never forgive myself for being found out. Seven times I've been pinched. Such carelessness! Embezzled some money, didn't you?

FLEMING: Quite a lot of money—over a long period. I gambled with my clients' investments, and for a time I made a profit for them. Then I lost, heavily. There was a crash. (*Pause*) And here I am.

DUKE: Hard luck, old man. (*Interestedly*) Are you thinking of going straight when you leave here?

FLEMING: At the moment, I'm pretty well ashamed of myself.

DUKE: You'll soon get over that. One thing prison does do for a man—it makes him utterly shameless.

FLEMING (*smiling sadly*): I've plenty of time for reflection. I can't begin to think about going out for a long time yet.

DUKE: Nonsense! You'll be thinking about it to-night. Nobody here thinks about anything else. Each man in this prison—in every prison—crosses off the days on a calendar—one by one.

FLEMING: Why?

DUKE: *Why?* Because the end of each day means more to a prisoner than to anyone else in the world. It means one day nearer freedom. (*Cheerfully*) I've only got 730 days left. Sounds better than two years. Hand over your jacket. (FLEMING *hands it to him, and he rolls it up, making it serve as a pillow*) You'll find that a help. These beds aren't too comfortable.

FLEMING (*quietly*): I don't imagine I'll get much sleep to-night. (*Half laughing*) Guilty conscience, I expect.

DUKE: Hard mattress—more likely! If you've

brought a conscience with you—you'll lose it. (*Chuckling*) Can't find mine anywhere. (*Pointing to hooks above bed*) Hang the rest of your things here. (*As* FLEMING *does so,* MORTON *appears in the doorway.*)

MORTON: 'Aven't you finished in 'ere yet? (*He comes into the cell and looks round.*)

DUKE: Just finished, sir.

MORTON: Get along to your own cell then.

DUKE (*as he goes out*): Yes, sir. Good night, sir.

MORTON (*to* FLEMING): Got everything you want?

This question strikes FLEMING *as absurd. He looks at his bare toes, then at* MORTON. *But the officer is not smiling.*

FLEMING: Yes. Thank you, sir.

MORTON *nods approval, and goes out, banging-to the door after him.* FLEMING *creeps into bed. He looks round the cell, then touches the trousers, waistcoat, etc., hanging above him. He shuts his eyes, and shudders.*

Suddenly the door opens again and MORTON *stands there.*

MORTON: Why aren't your shoes outside?

FLEMING: Oh, I forgot.

There is a long pause.

MORTON (*shouting*): Well, put 'em outside then. And be quick about it!

FLEMING *jumps out of bed and does as he is told. When he returns to the cell,* MORTON *just glares at him, then goes out, banging door.* FLEMING *stands motionless, staring into space. Then his eyes close and his head falls forward.*

BLACK OUT

The light goes up on RUDGE, *who, dressed in shirt and trousers, is sitting on his chair doing sums on a slate. The bed is made up and in a slightly different position from the one it occupied in the previous scene.*

RUDGE (*to himself*) : Over a thousand blinkin' days in this ruddy hole. Strewth!

The door is unlocked and SAUNDERS *enters.*

SAUNDERS (*pleasantly*) : Mr. Rudge, isn't it?

RUDGE (*rising*) : That's me name. What can I do for you, sir?

SAUNDERS (*rather taken aback*) : Well, I was about to ask you the same question!

RUDGE (*pointing to chair*) : Take a seat?

SAUNDERS : Then where will you sit?

RUDGE : The bed will do me, though we ain't supposed to use it except to sleep on. (*Throws himself down on it*) This place is all rules, and not a bit of sense in any of 'em, so far as I can see.

SAUNDERS (*sitting down*) : This isn't your first — visit here?

RUDGE : Bless yer, no! I've been in and outer these places a few times. Never 'ad such a long stretch as this one, though. Five years! Makes yer think, don't it?

SAUNDERS (*interested*) : What, exactly, does it make you think?

RUDGE : Why, what a fool I've been.

SAUNDERS : To realise one's own folly, is a step in the right direction. Experience teaches us wisdom in the end.

RUDGE : You're right. I shan't never mix meself up with another smash-and-grab raid. Not likely.

SAUNDERS : The game's not worth the candle ?

RUDGE : It's not. I oughter stuck to honest burglary. That's my job, and I know it from A to Z.

SAUNDERS : Oh, I see.

RUDGE : Smash-and-grab is all right for youngsters. But not at my age. I'm too old to start mucking about with new games. 'Aven't got the nerve, for one thing.

SAUNDERS : It needs nerve, I suppose ?

RUDGE : Oh, it does. And you 'ave to be that quick ! Everything timed to the minute. A nervy business. I was properly caught, and the others with me. My fault, too. I'll tell you what 'appened. I was in charge of the car, see ? I 'ad to drive the others away when they'd got the stuff, see ? Well, there was I, waiting with the engine all started up, ready to drive like hell the minute the others got in. See ?

SAUNDERS (*nodding*) : Yes.

RUDGE : Well, I did drive like hell. Only the others 'adn't got in ! I'd started a second too soon, and the others was left standing on the pavement, with piles of fur coats on their arms. Was they angry with me when they got caught ! Can't blame 'em, can you ?

SAUNDERS (*not quite knowing what to say*) : It seems to have been an unfortunate business altogether.

RUDGE : You've said it. Very unfortunate. And Mrs. Rudge didn't half turn sour on me. Fair lemony, she was ! Angry ? Worse than a couple of cops. You see, from the first, she'd warned me not to play with new ideas, but to stick to what I knew. And she was right.

SAUNDERS : Have you any children, Rudge ?

RUDGE : One boy, sir. A good lad. I've great hopes of 'im.

SAUNDERS : Where is he now ?

RUDGE : Rochester, sir.

SAUNDERS : At school ?

RUDGE (*smiling*) : Call it that if you like. But it's really Borstal.

SAUNDERS : I'm sorry to hear your boy's been in trouble, too. (*Encouragingly*) But you know, Borstal may make a man of him.

RUDGE : It depends whether 'e gets in with the right set, or not. That's the trouble with them places.

SAUNDERS : They've turned out some pretty good men.

RUDGE : Your humble servant amongst them.

SAUNDERS : Were you at Borstal ?

RUDGE : Right in at the start, I was—way back in nineteen oh eight. I learned me profession there. Proper lads, we was. And I think my boy will take after his dad. (*Admiringly*) He's pretty tough, is Jim. Slick, too.

By this time SAUNDERS *really is a little embarrassed. He is uncertain what attitude to take.* RUDGE *sees this, and immediately adopts an almost fatherly attitude towards him.*

Don't let my talk upset you, sir.

SAUNDERS : You present a rather puzzling case, Rudge.

RUDGE : I suppose I do, to you, sir. But you don't 'ave to worry about me. I'm a waste of any chaplain's time, I am. God, and repentance, and all that—it don't wash with me. Never 'as, and never will. Some men in this prison will be glad of your help.

You'll be able to do something for them, I shouldn't wonder. But not for me, sir. I'm 'wide,' I am ; and so long as there's suckers in this world, I'll go on being wide.

SAUNDERS (*rising*) : At least you're frank about yourself, Rudge.

RUDGE : I know meself pretty well. Ought to, at my time of life. Thank you for coming to see me, all the same, sir.

SAUNDERS : That's all right. (*He moves towards the door.*)

RUDGE : Sir !

SAUNDERS (*turning*) : What is it ?

RUDGE : There's something I'd be glad if you would do for me.

SAUNDERS : And what is that ?

RUDGE : It would make my life here a lot brighter, and I'd really be very grateful to you, if you'd let me know the football results on Saturday nights.

SAUNDERS : I'll remember, Rudge.

RUDGE (*taking up his slate again*) : God bless yer, sir.

BLACK OUT

The light goes up on PORTER, *who, fully dressed, but wearing his felt slippers, is standing on his chair, which he has placed beneath the window. He has his face pressed against it, trying to see into the darkness. So absorbed is he, that he does not notice the entrance of the* GOVERNOR, *who stands watching him. The* GOVERNOR *coughs to attract attention.* PORTER, *swings round as if he had been shot ; fear in his eyes.*

PORTER : Please, sir, I was just trying to see outside.

GOVERNOR : And it was too dark to see anything ?

PORTER (*timidly*) : I didn't mean any harm, sir.

GOVERNOR : I'm sure you didn't—Porter. James Porter—that's your name, isn't it ?

PORTER (*climbing down from the chair*) : Yes, sir.

GOVERNOR (*reflectively*) : Let me see, where are we ? D Hall. Yes. From that window, in the daytime, you can look out over the garden. We're very proud of our garden, you know. Are you interested in that sort of thing ?

PORTER : I had a garden at home, sir. Just a small one. In the summer I used to spend quite a bit of time there, getting it to look nice. My wife and the daughter—they'd help me.

Mentioning his wife and daughter upsets PORTER, *who has been on the verge of tears since he entered the prison. The* GOVERNOR *is aware of this, and does his best to comfort him.*

GOVERNOR : We might be able to find you work to do in the garden here. Would you like that ?

PORTER : Thank you, sir. I should.

There is a pause. PORTER *looks about as pathetic as a man can look.*

GOVERNOR : You mustn't let this thing get you down too much, Porter. I know how you're feeling. Pretty rotten. You think everybody here's against you. But they're not, you know.

PORTER (*who has been staring at his feet, looking up*) : It's not about myself I'm worrying, sir. Honestly it's not. But my wife ; and Lily—that's my daughter—it's so terrible for them.

GOVERNOR (*nods understandingly*): I know. The relations and friends of the men here suffer just as much as the men themselves. More, sometimes. The only thing is for everyone to put as brave a face on it as possible. That's what you must do.

PORTER: It's not easy, sir.

GOVERNOR: Do you think I don't know that? In my time I've seen some desperately unhappy men. But I've seen some brave ones, too. (*Putting a hand on his shoulder*) What you've got to do is to pull yourself together. See?

PORTER: In the papers, sir, when my trial was on, they made me out to be much worse than I am. I did wrong, I know; but really I didn't realise how serious it was. I never stopped to think—about what I was doing. I only thought of how much I wanted the money, and of what the money would do for my wife. (*Pause*) I kept thinking of her, and of what the doctor had said.

GOVERNOR: What is the matter with your wife?

PORTER: They don't seem to know, sir.

GOVERNOR: I see. I'm sorry.

PORTER: At first, when the men came and offered me money to get hold of those papers for them, I wouldn't listen. I told them they'd mistaken their man. But they came again and again. And in the end I did listen. I didn't know what was in the papers—that they contained information likely to be useful to an enemy country. But I knew where they were kept, and how to get them for a few hours. And because of the money, that I wanted for my wife, I did—what I did.

GOVERNOR : You abused a position of trust. That's all the law can take into account. But I see how it was, Porter. I'm sorry for you.

PORTER (*desperately*) : Some of the papers called me a spy. But I was never that. I was weak, and I did wrong. But really I wasn't a spy, sir. Really!

GOVERNOR : Of course you weren't. Mrs. Porter will be coming to visit you, I expect. You've got that to look forward to.

PORTER : If she's well enough, and has the money for the fare, she'll come. Nothing would stop her. She's always been such a good wife—and for me to have brought this disgrace on her, and on Lily, my daughter . . .

PORTER *is obviously about to break down, when the* GOVERNOR, *as if he were dealing with a child, takes him by the shoulders and shakes him gently.*

GOVERNOR : Come, Porter—keep a hold on yourself. Nothing is ever as bad as it seems to be. Your wife wouldn't want you to give way. I'm sure she's being very brave about all this. You're not going to let her down, are you?

For a second PORTER *appears to be giving in, but with a tremendous effort he controls himself.*

PORTER (*standing apart*) : I'm sorry, sir.

GOVERNOR : That's all right. I'll be seeing you in the morning, and then we'll arrange for you to work with the gardeners. You'll find plenty to occupy your mind.

PORTER : Thank you, sir.

GOVERNOR (*as he goes out*) : Good night, Porter. Get some sleep.

PORTER: Good night, sir.

As the door closes, PORTER *runs up to it. He feels its surface with his hands, a gesture which emphasises how shut in he is. Then he crosses the cell and sits down on his chair.*

BLACK OUT

END OF ACT I

ACT II

SCENE I

SCENE: *Outside the cells: eighteen months later. This is a part of the ground corridor of the prison. The doors of three cells are visible. Each cell has a round peep-hole at the level of a man's eye. On the wall, close to each cell door, hangs a square board with prisoner's name, number, and record. Overhead is just seen the iron structure of the first-floor corridor. Also, on the wall, hangs a slate, on which the number of prisoners present is chalked.*

At the back, centre, sits BATES, *his cap over one eye, and his tunic unbottoned, trying to get some sleep. In front of him are seated* RUDGE, PORTER, DUKE *and* BATS *—all sewing mail-bags.* FLEMING *is slowly scrubbing the floor throughout the scene, and has with him a bucket of water for that purpose. Being a hot afternoon, the men have their jackets off, and have hung them on the backs of their chairs.*

DUKE (*affectedly, holding out his work*): When I'm free, I never see a postman's bag without wondering if it was one I worked on in prison. Strange, isn't it?

RUDGE (*imitating his voice*): Oh, very strange! (*In his natural voice*) I never see a copper without wanting to bash his ruddy 'ead in.

BATES (*whose eyes are only half open*) : If you men must talk, for God's sake pipe down. With the row you're making I can't get a wink of sleep.

FLEMING (*to* BATES) : Did you have a bad night, sir ?

BATES : Bad night ! I never closed me eyes once. Howling the whole time, the kid was. Sometimes I wish I was a single man again.

RUDGE : You ever 'ad any kids, Duke ?

DUKE : Not that I'm aware of.

RUDGE : Lucky for them. I should go on being careful if I was you.

DUKE : The question is unlikely to arise in the future.

RUDGE : How's that ?

DUKE : I'm forsaking bigamy. My health will no longer stand it.

PORTER : It's the food they give us here that ruins the health.

RUDGE : You've said it, Jim. Badly cooked, too. Not that I couldn't do with a bit more of it. I get that hungry. Sometimes my stomach thinks my throat's been cut.

PORTER : I haven't had a proper meal in the eighteen months I've been here. Except Christmas day. That was all right. My wife will see a difference in me, I'm afraid.

DUKE : She's coming to visit you this afternoon, isn't she ?

PORTER : Yes. For the first time. She's been too ill to come before. It will be wonderful, seeing her again. Wonderful.

RUDGE (*morosely*) : My old girl's coming to see me this afternoon.

FLEMING : You don't sound exactly bucked by the idea.

RUDGE : I can't say I am, really.

FLEMING : That's odd, isn't it ?

RUDGE : You don't know Mrs. Rudge. Kind of funny, she is. Moody—like. Sweet as sugar one minute—and like hell let loose the next. Very upsetting for a chap.

DUKE : It must be.

BATS, *who works away on his own, taking no notice of the others, suddenly starts to hum, 'Oh God our Help in Ages Past.' They all stare at him.*

RUDGE : Now the Salvation Army's started off. For Gawd's sake . . .

FLEMING : Let him sing his hymns, they don't do any harm.

RUDGE : The judge didn't include that in my sentence.

PORTER (*looking left*) : The Governor's coming.

RUDGE *immediately throws his scissors into* BATES' *lap, waking him up with a start.*

BATES : What the bleeding . . .

RUDGE (*in a loud whisper*) : Governor !

BATES *buttons his tunic and stands to attention.* BATS *ceases humming. The men work in silence. Enter* GOVERNOR.

BATES (*saluting*) : Five present—all correct, sir !

GOVERNOR (*to* BATES) : Warm afternoon, isn't it ?

BATES : Very warm, sir.

The GOVERNOR *passes on. There is a general sigh of relief when he has gone.*

Phew ! That was a close shave.

RUDGE (*to* BATES): Was you 'aving a nice dream?

BATES (*preparing to settle down again*): You get on with your work, unless you want to lose marks.

RUDGE (*hurt*): All right. No need to get shirty.

For a few seconds the men work in a silence broken only by the low humming of BATS. FIELD *enters, quietly. He looks at* BATES, *whose eyes are closed, and then at the men—all sharing the joke together. Then* FIELD *goes up to him, and flicks his nose.* BATES *jumps up, crying out.*)

BATES: Who did that? (*Sees* FIELD) Oh, it's you. (*In a sing-song voice*) Five present—all correct, sir.

FIELD: Having a nice nap, sir.

BATES (*in an injured tone*): If you'd been kept awake half the night by a howling kid . . .

FIELD (*soothingly*): All right, old man; I'm not going to report you. Half the prison's asleep this afternoon. Must be the hot weather. I want Bats and Toff.

BATS *and* FLEMING *stand up.*

BATES: You can have 'em—with pleasure. (*He rubs the figure 'five' off the slate, and in its place chalks up 'three.'*)

FIELD (*to* BATS *and* FLEMING): You two men can get on with that mending job on my roof. Hurry, now. I'll meet you by the big gate.

BATS *hurries out, but* FLEMING *stays to put his bucket aside, and roll down his sleeves.*

(*To* FLEMING) I dare say my wife will have a bit of extra grub for you, Toff. I'll speak to her.

FLEMING: Thank you very much, sir.

FIELD: Come along. (*Over his shoulder, to* BATES) Pleasant dreams! (*Exit, followed by* FLEMING.)

After a short silence, when he has made sure that BATES *isn't listening to him*, RUDGE *speaks quietly*.

RUDGE: Nice job that, for the Toff—mending Mr. Field's roof. Convenient, too.

DUKE: Can't say I should care for it myself. (*Looking at his hands*) As it is, my hands are in a frightful state. No, manual labour does not appeal to me.

RUDGE: I don't suppose it *appeals* to the Toff. (*Mysteriously*) But then it wasn't the work I was thinking about.

DUKE: I'm afraid I don't follow you.

RUDGE (*moving his chair nearer*): A little bird told me that the Toff and Mrs. Field . . .

DUKE: I don't believe a word of it. (*Interested*) How long's this been going on?

RUDGE: Can't say, exactly—but they've been a ruddy long time mending that roof.

DUKE (*nodding*): They have been a long time. But what about Mr. Field? Doesn't he know?

RUDGE: He can't know yet. But he'll find out. Some men was talking about it in the carpenter's shop yesterday. Somebody's sure to tell him. Somebody always does tell 'usbands them kind of things, don't they?

DUKE: That's right. (*After a pause*) I don't blame them, do you?

RUDGE: Who?

DUKE: The Toff and Mrs. Field.

RUDGE: Oh, well, I don't hold with promiscuity. (*amusingly pronounced*) Not outside, that is. But in here, things is rather different.

DUKE: Very different. (*Getting quite pleased with the idea*) They're good-lookers, both of them. And Mrs.

Field is the only attractive woman in the place. I've always said so. Lovely girl, she is.

RUDGE: It's only natural they should 'ave a bit of fun, when you come to think of it.

DUKE: Oh, I agree. It's unnatural, the life we're made to live here. Most unnatural. It encourages men to be vicious. Look what goes on . . .

RUDGE (*nodding*): I've seen a thing or two going on here, I must say.

DUKE: Yet they send men to prison for behaving like that. I don't understand it at all.

RUDGE: There's a lot we don't understand.

DUKE: Somebody ought to do something about it, though.

RUDGE: Ah! Now you're talking. But nobody never does nothing.

DUKE (*unable to leave the subject*): The Toff—and Mrs. Field . . . (*Suddenly*) What kind of woman do you particularly admire, Rudge?

RUDGE (*after thought*): Plump—with a bust.

DUKE: Is your wife like that?

RUDGE: No. Flat as a pancake fore and aft!

DUKE: Pity.

RUDGE: Tragedy!

DUKE: A woman I knew once, had such . . .

Enter MORTON.

MORTON: 2046. Rudge—here?

RUDGE (*rising*): That's me, sir.

MORTON: You're to come for your visit. Your wife's here to see you.

BATES (*monotonously, as he changes figures on the slate*): All correct, sir, five—and three away.

MORTON: Right, sir.

PORTER (*to* MORTON) : I'm to have a visit to-day, sir.

MORTON : All right. Nobody said you hadn't. It's not three o'clock yet. Your turn will come.

PORTER : Yes, sir.

MORTON (*to* RUDGE) : Come along. Look sharp.

RUDGE (*to* DUKE) : Wish me luck !

Exit RUDGE *and* MORTON.

DUKE (*to* PORTER) : I don't think Rudge is too anxious to see his wife. I should say there is a certain incompatability of temperament between them.

PORTER : I've been looking forward to my visit ever since I've been here. Do they really only give you thirty minutes ?

DUKE : That is the official time. But if there's a decent screw on duty, you get a bit extra sometimes.

PORTER (*sadly*) : I expect Mrs. Porter *will* see a difference in me. And then, everyone looks different in these clothes. I hope I don't forget all the things I want to ask her. I feel quite nervous. Funny, isn't it ? (*Thinking that perhaps he is talking too much about himself*) Doesn't anybody ever come to visit you, Duke ?

DUKE (*shaking his head*) : In my case, it would be unwise. Once two of my wives turned up at the same time. They didn't get on at all well together. (*Pause*) One of them had to be taken to the hospital afterwards. (*Sighing*) Sweet, foolish creatures, women !

A deep snore comes from BATES.

CURTAIN

Scene 2

Scene: *The parlour of* Field's *house.*

The furniture is old-fashioned and ugly. The walls are covered with patterned wallpaper. There are one or two cheap pictures and framed photographs: family portraits and groups.

On the table there is a sewing-machine, work-basket, some cut-out pieces of material, etc.

Mary Field *is looking out of the window. She is a country-bred girl of about twenty-seven, not strikingly pretty, but attractive in a quiet way.*

She stands to one side of the window so that she cannot be seen from outside. She goes to the door, opens it a few inches and listens: then goes to the table and begins working with the sewing-machine.

After a few moments Field *comes in.*

Field: Hallo, my dear. Working?

Mary: Hallo.

Field: I've brought Bats and the Toff over. They've gone up to finish off that job on the roof.

Mary (*stops turning the handle of the sewing-machine*): To finish it?

Field: They ought to get through with it to-day or to-morrow.

Mary: I thought it would take longer than that.

Field: It may do. They always make the most of these outside jobs. Spend twice as long on them as they need. I don't blame them. Makes a change.

MARY : Yes ; they must be glad of a change. Mrs. Baker was telling me some of them go a bit funny in the head, when they've been inside a long time. Like Bats.

FIELD : It gets most of them in the end. Just a kink somewhere.

MARY : How long does it take for that to happen ?

FIELD : Depends. Some go sooner than others.

MARY : How long is it as a rule ? Five years ?

FIELD : It's not so much how many years they've been in that counts. It's how many they've got in front of them.

MARY : Then it's only the ones with very long sentences ?

FIELD : Usually. Some of them go to Broadmoor when their sentences are up.

MARY : That's horrible ! To keep them here all that time, and then when they ought to be free again, to send them there.

FIELD : Couldn't send them out into the world if they're crazy. Wouldn't be fair on them.

MARY : But if they're as bad as that they ought to be sent to Broadmoor earlier. Not kept here, in prison, till the end of their sentences.

FIELD : Oh, well. It's none of my business. (*Picks up a piece of material*) What are you making ?

MARY : A new dress.

FIELD : What, another one ?

MARY : You want me to look nice, don't you ?

FIELD : You look all right to me whatever you wear.

MARY : You should be very glad I make my own dresses. It saves money.

FIELD: I think I'll go over and see Baker. Those two will be all right up on the roof.

MARY: You oughtn't to leave them, really.

FIELD: I won't be long. I thought you might give the Toff a bit of food. If you've got anything to spare.

MARY: Why only him? Bats might like something too.

FIELD: He wouldn't take it. Bats has got some idea that God will be angry with him if he does anything against the regulations. He says he's got to expiate his own sin before he can go out and lead others to the straight and narrow path. It saves us a lot of trouble. Makes him a model prisoner. I told the Toff you might have something for him. He'll come down when he sees me go. (*He goes out.*)

MARY *goes to a mirror and tidies herself; then she goes back to the sewing-machine and begins working again.* FLEMING *comes in.* MARY *continues to work. He puts his hand on her shoulder. She takes his hand, presses it to her cheek and kisses it.*

MARY: My darling. (*She turns her face up to him and he bends down and kisses her on the lips.*)

FLEMING: How long will he be?

MARY: I don't know. He didn't say. I'm afraid he'll be back soon.

FLEMING: He told me to come down and see if you'd got anything for me to eat.

MARY: Shall I fetch you something?

FLEMING: No. Perhaps we've only got a few moments. We mustn't waste them.

MARY: He said you'd nearly finished that job on the roof. Does it mean you won't be coming here any more?

FLEMING: We shan't finish it to-day.

MARY: But to-morrow . . . he said you'd get through with it to-day or to-morrow. Can't you take longer? You must!

FLEMING (*soothingly*): My darling . . .

MARY: He wouldn't mind. He said they always take as long as possible over outside jobs.

FLEMING: Most of them do. But it's different with Bats. He does everything he should and nothing he shouldn't. That's what happens when you get religion.

MARY: But can't you do something? You must think of something. I can't bear it if I'm not going to see you again.

FLEMING: My darling, you mustn't cry. We've only got a few moments.

MARY (*almost hysterically*): But we've got to think of something!

FLEMING (*Taking her to the settee*): Come here, and sit by me.

MARY: We'll be together always one day, won't we? Always. I must think of that. Otherwise I'll go mad. He—slept with me last night.

FLEMING: You're making me feel that I've only brought you misery. If we'd never seen each other . . .

MARY (*putting her hand over his mouth*): You're not to say that! Perhaps I never loved him. I think I only married him to get away from home.

FLEMING: I hate deceiving him in this way. He's been so good to me.

MARY: He's like that to them all.

FLEMING: He's gone out of his way to be kind to me. All sorts of little things.

MARY: That can't be helped. You mustn't think of it.

FLEMING: I like him, and I wish I hated him.

MARY: Doesn't it make you hate him—to think of him and me together?

FLEMING: No. I can't hate him for that.

MARY: When he touches me, I want to . . . It makes me feel so . . . I can't explain. Last night . . . when he . . . It was horrible! I was so happy before, thinking of you . . . how you'd kissed me and held me in your arms. And then I had to . . . pretend . . . . with him.

FLEMING: My darling . . .

MARY: And I've got to go on pretending for more than three years! Last night I thought I'd leave him and go away, and wait for you alone. But I'd never see you then. As long as I stay here I shall see you sometimes. I think I can endure anything for that.

FLEMING: I'm making you so unhappy.

MARY: No, that's not true. It's only through you that I know what happiness can be like. I used to think about it, and read about it in books, and wonder what it felt like. Now I know. I'm *not* happy. I can never be happy until we're together. But I know what happiness is.

FLEMING: Perhaps it's better not to know.

MARY: Not for us. Because we love each other. We can make it all come true. Can't we? (*He kisses her*) How many women have you loved?

FLEMING (*smiling*): What do you want me to say?

MARY: I want you to tell me the truth.

FLEMING: Are you sure?

MARY: You must never lie to me. We belong to

each other. (*afraid*) How many women have you loved?

FLEMING (*slowly*): I've never loved anyone.

MARY (*kisses him*): Derek. My dear. What sort of clothes do you wear? I've only seen you in these.

FLEMING: Why; just ordinary clothes.

MARY: I want to know exactly what they're like. What kind of suits, and ties, and shirts. I expect you're very fussy about how you look.

FLEMING: I don't think I am.

MARY: Do you have your clothes made for you?

FLEMING: Only my suits. I usually get other things ready-made.

MARY: What other things?

FLEMING: Well, shirts and shoes . . .

MARY: D'you mean to say some men have their shoes made specially for them?

FLEMING: Yes.

MARY: I should have thought only a man with a club-foot would need to do that. How much do they cost?

FLEMING: Depends what shop you get them from. About four or five guineas, as a rule.

MARY: Five guineas for a pair of shoes! Have you ever paid that?

FLEMING: Sometimes. It's cheaper in the long run.

MARY: Did you need money very badly when you . . .

FLEMING: Don't let's talk about that now.

MARY: If you hadn't done it, I'd never have seen you. It's funny that. I can't imagine what it would be like without you. I've forgotten what I used to think about. I go to sleep thinking about you. And sometimes when I wake up in the morning I'm still thinking of you, as if I haven't been asleep at all. But some morning's it's different. I wake up and think of other things for a few moments. And then I know that something wonderful has happened, and I can't remember what it is. And then suddenly it all comes back. It's lovely when it's like that.

FLEMING: I think of you, too. Nearly all the time.

MARY: Does it make it easier for you?

FLEMING: Yes.

MARY: I'm glad. It must have been terrible for you at first.

FLEMING: It's like a nightmare that goes on and on. D'you know how it is when you're sleeping in a strange place and you wake up and don't know where you are?

MARY: Yes.

FLEMING: I used to do that at first. And then I'd realise . . . all the horror of it . . . That was the worst moment of the day. Sometimes now I wake up from a dream, and I think . . . (*He breaks down and buries his face in her lap.*)

MARY: Don't cry, my dear. One day it will all be over. I shall always love you. And you'll forget this.

FLEMING: The time goes so slowly. I never knew time could go so slowly.

MARY: But it's better now, isn't it? You've got me. I'm waiting for you. We've got so much to look forward to. And until then, we'll see each other sometimes. It may not be very often, but now and then . . . I tell you what we'll do—we'll fix a time every day when we'll think of each other. I shall be thinking of you nearly all the time, but that'll be a special moment. You'll know for certain then that

I'm thinking of you, and I'll know that you're thinking of me. Shall we do that ?

FLEMING : Yes. In the evening. When I'm shut up for the night. That'll be the best time. At eight o'clock.

MARY : Every evening at eight o'clock.

FLEMING : But you may not be able to. You might be anywhere. Other people in the room.

MARY : I'll always try and be alone. But it won't matter if I'm not. Even if I'm talking to somebody, I'll still think of you. I'll never fail you. I promise.

FLEMING : We'll share that moment. It will belong to us both. Something to hold on to. You know, I'm afraid at times—of what may happen.

MARY : What d'you mean ?

FLEMING : I'm afraid I may not be strong enough. I feel terribly small, and everything else is so big. Even the other men. They're like giants. And the walls are so high. They go right up into the clouds.

MARY : No, darling. No. They're only very little walls.

FLEMING : They're high. And thick. So thick that they can't hear you on the other side. I could go on shouting and shouting, but they'd never hear.

MARY : I shall hear you. There's nothing to be afraid of. I shall hear you.

FLEMING : Will you ?

MARY : Of course, darling. You've only got to whisper, and I shall hear you.

FLEMING : Will you ? Are you sure ?

MARY : Quite sure.

FLEMING : I'm so glad. I was afraid nobody would

hear. It's terrible when you're quite alone. And you're locked up. The walls come so close together.

MARY: Look at me, darling. Look into my eyes. (*He does so*) You mustn't forget that I'm waiting for you. You won't forget that, will you?

FLEMING: Suppose I can't reach you?

MARY: You can if you try.

FLEMING: I love you so very much. (*He puts his arm round her, and his head against her breast.*)

MARY: You'll think of me every evening, won't you? Every evening at eight o'clock. Whenever you think of me, I shall be with you. And then you'll be safe. There'll be nothing to be afraid of.

FLEMING: You're all I've got. I love you.

The door opens quietly. BATS *comes in.* MARY *hears something, looks round, and gives a little involuntary gasp.* FLEMING *looks up and sees him. For a moment all three are quite motionless.*

MARY: What are you doing down here? (*She rises*) Why aren't you working? How dare you come into my room!

BATS (*with his eyes fixed on her*): You should have locked the door. It was locked the other time.

MARY: What are you talking about? What other time?

BATS: When I found the other two together. They'd locked the door. But I broke it open.

MARY: Yes, that's all right, Bats. Now you'd better go back and get on with your work. (*To* FLEMING) You'd better go with him.

FLEMING (*going to the door; to* BATS): I've been having something to eat. Field said I could.

BATS: Go on.

Fleming *looks at* Mary. *She signals to him to go. He hesitates for a moment and goes out.* Bats *stands looking at* Mary.

Bats: Jezebel!

Mary: You'd better go.

Bats: God sees everything. You can't hide anything from Him.

Mary: If you don't go at once, I'll tell my husband about this.

Bats: Maybe there's something else you'd better tell him. (*He walks slowly towards her with his eyes fixed on her face. She steps back.*)

Mary: There's nothing. I swear to you, there's nothing! (*She tries to run past him to the door. He catches her by the wrist and holds her*) Let me go!

Bats: I'll not hurt you. The other one tried to run away, too. I put my hands round her neck, and I squeezed it until there wasn't a breath left in her body. A little string of beads, she was wearing. They broke and rolled over the floor. I oughtn't to have done it. God doesn't allow us to take His judgment into our own hands.

Mary: Then you won't say anything, will you? That wouldn't be right. God might be angry with you again.

Bats (*nods his head, releases her, and goes to the door. He turns and shouts*): You're all alike. You harlot!

Curtain

SCENE 3

SCENE: *A visiting-room. It is quite bare, except for a deal table and three chairs. There are two doors, right and left.*

The door on the right opens and MORTON *comes in, followed by* MRS. RUDGE.

MORTON: You mustn't give him anything, and you must keep . . .

MRS. RUDGE: All right, all right! You can't tell me nothing, young fellow. I was visiting my old man in quod when you was no more than a little nappie-soaker!

MORTON: You keep a civil tongue . . .

MRS. RUDGE (*in a stentorian voice*): Shut up! (MORTON *is silenced*) That gave you a jerk, didn't it? Used to doing all the shouting yourself, aren't you? Don't like it when it's the other way round, do you? Is you ma alive?

MORTON: What business is that of yours?

MRS. RUDGE: 'Cos if she is I hope she's bloody well ashamed of you! Catch any son of mine being a dirty, sneaking screw.

MORTON: That's enough of that!

MRS. RUDGE: You do your job and fetch my old man and make it slippy, see, or I'll have something to say to the Governor about you.

MORTON *goes out left. After a few seconds he returns with* RUDGE. *During the following scene* MORTON *stands a short distance behind the table.*

MORTON (*indicating a chair to* RUDGE) : Sit there.

MRS. RUDGE : He knows where to sit. (*She and* RUDGE *sit on opposite sides of the table*) How are you, Bill ?

RUDGE : All right. Where d'you get the 'at, Mabel ?

MRS. RUDGE : Like me in it ?

RUDGE : Suits you.

MRS. RUDGE : Ought to. Paid thirty bob for it.

RUDGE : Where d'you get the dough ?

MRS. RUDGE : Dug it up in the back garden.

MORTON : None of that !

MRS. RUDGE : None of what ?

MORTON : You know.

MRS. RUDGE : What's the matter with you ?

MORTON : You know you're not allowed to talk in code.

MRS. RUDGE : Talk in code ! Who's talking in code ?

MORTON : You are. ' Dug it up in the back garden.'

MRS. RUDGE : Smart, ain't he ?

RUDGE : How are you keeping, Mabel ?

MRS. RUDGE : O.K. Things is all right. I've been seeing a bit of Freddie lately.

RUDGE : You didn't ought to, Mabel.

MRS. RUDGE : Why not ?

RUDGE : It ain't safe.

MRS. RUDGE : Got to live, ain't I ? You didn't leave me exactly well-provided for, did you ? Can't live on air, can I ?

RUDGE : Freddie's way ain't the only way.

MRS. RUDGE : It's the way that suits me.

RUDGE : Nice of you to come and see me, Mabel.

MRS. RUDGE : Does me good to see your ugly old mug. Even though it 'as cost me fifteen and nine-pence. You're looking well, I must say.

RUDGE : I may look all right . . .

MRS. RUDGE : Now then, I didn't come all this way to hear you grumble.

RUDGE : Who's grumbling ?

MRS. RUDGE : Nobody yet. I went down to Rochester last week to see Jim.

RUDGE : How is he ?

MRS. RUDGE : Fine. You won't know him. Sprung up like a beanstalk this last year. Taller than you now.

RUDGE : Is he ?

MRS. RUDGE : And he can run. I went down for the sports day. Lovely, it was. Jim won the hundred yards. Won it easy.

RUDGE : Won the hundred yards, did he ? That's the stuff. I told him to go in for the short distances. More useful to him later.

MRS. RUDGE : And he won the long jump.

RUDGE : No !

MRS. RUDGE : He did. Lovely jumper ; oh, he's a lovely jumper. Don't wobble when he lands.

RUDGE : That's the way. That's what you want.

MRS. RUDGE : He got a prize for both.

RUDGE : I don't care about the prizes. It'll be useful to him in his career. That's what counts.

MRS. RUDGE : I know. Still, it was nice to see him go up and get his prizes. I felt real proud of him.

RUDGE : Wish I'd been there. Good old Jim.

MRS. RUDGE : He asked them to let him have your old cell. But they wouldn't.

RUDGE: Swine! They ain't got no feeling.

MRS. RUDGE: 'Ard-'earted devils!

RUDGE: Be nice for the boy to be in his dad's old cell. Wouldn't do them any harm.

MRS. RUDGE: Course it wouldn't.

RUDGE: I'm glad he's doing well. I did well when I was there. Course they didn't have no sports in my time. Nothing like that. But you know, Mabel, looking back on it now, I think they was the happiest days of my life!

MRS. RUDGE: That's a nice thing to say to your wife!

RUDGE: Oh, well, you know what I mean. Not counting our honeymoon.

MRS. RUDGE: D'you know what I been thinking, Bill?

RUDGE: No. What?

MRS. RUDGE: I thought if I could manage to put a bit by, just a few pounds, d'you know what I thought I'd do with it?

RUDGE: No?

MRS. RUDGE: I thought when you come out, you and me, we might go to Brighton again, just for a week or two. We've never been since then.

RUDGE: That's an idea! Only you could have thought of that, Mabel. It'd be lovely.

MRS. RUDGE: Do you good, too. Set you up again. Nothing like a dose from Doctor Brighton when you've done a stretch.

RUDGE: D'you think you'll be able to manage it?

MRS. RUDGE: Well, I can't tell now, can I? Things is all right at present. They may be different in three years' time.

RUDGE: You're a sport, Mabel. Tell me what you've been doing, apart from (*with a glance at* MORTON) you know what.

MRS. RUDGE: Nothing much. Oh, d'you hear about Clipper?

RUDGE: No. What?

MRS. RUDGE: Silly old fool!

RUDGE: What's he done?

MRS. RUDGE: Tried a big job on his own. Thought he'd show us all.

RUDGE: What happened?

MRS. RUDGE: What d'you think?

RUDGE: How long did he get?

MRS. RUDGE: Seven.

RUDGE: Hell and bloody scissors!

MRS. RUDGE: And it's Dartmoor.

RUDGE: The bastards! Old Clipper in Dartmoor. He'll never stand it. He won't come out.

MRS. RUDGE: That's what Spike said.

RUDGE: How's Spike?

MRS. RUDGE: Same as usual.

RUDGE: Poor old Clipper.

MRS. RUDGE: Well, it was his own fault.

RUDGE: It's good to see you again, Mabel.

MRS. RUDGE: I quite miss you, you know.

RUDGE: Don't miss me too much.

MRS. RUDGE: Why not?

RUDGE: You might get lonely and try someone else.

MRS. RUDGE: P'raps I have.

RUDGE: Go on!

MRS. RUDGE: What's the grub like?

RUDGE: Lousy!

MRS. RUDGE: Never mind.

RUDGE: Oh, was it?

MRS. RUDGE: Yes, it was.

RUDGE: You can spend thirty bob on an 'at . . .

MRS. RUDGE: It's my money, ain't it?

RUDGE: But you can't afford fifteen and nine to come and see your old man what's got himself in trouble . . .

MRS. RUDGE: I have come, ain't I? Here I am!

RUDGE: Here you are, all right. No mistake about that.

MRS. RUDGE: And a fine welcome I get!

RUDGE: And I suppose you think it does me good to hear your blasted old nagging tongue for half an hour, you . . .

MRS. RUDGE: Don't you swear at me, you snotty-nosed bastard!

MORTON: Pipe down! Pipe down, both of you!

MRS. RUDGE (*turning on him*): You mind your own business, see!

MORTON: Don't you talk to me like that!

MRS. RUDGE: I'll talk to you how I please!

RUDGE: Now then, Mabel, it don't do no good . . .

MRS. RUDGE (*to* MORTON): Don't interfere, see! I come here to talk to my husband, and I'll talk to him how I like.

MORTON: You talk to him quiet, or you won't talk to him at all.

RUDGE: How's old Bottle, Mabel?

MRS. RUDGE: Old Bottle? Oh, he's all right.

RUDGE: Still at it, eh?

MRS. RUDGE: Still at it.

RUDGE: What about Tom? How's young Tom?

MRS. RUDGE: All right.

RUDGE : And Judy ?

MRS. RUDGE : All right.

RUDGE : You *have* got a lot to tell me.

MRS. RUDGE : Telling you everything you ask, ain't I ?

RUDGE : All right !

MRS. RUDGE : I come all the way down here, thinking you'll be glad to see me. 'Poor old Bill,' I says to myself, 'he must be getting a bit down in the mouth,' and this is all the thanks I get for it.

RUDGE : Well, I said I was glad to see you, didn't I ?

MRS. RUDGE : I suppose you think I like being a ruddy grass widow for five bleeding years ! And me in my prime of life !

RUDGE : Aw, shut up !

MRS. RUDGE : It ain't good for any woman being alone all that time. It ain't natural.

RUDGE : I can't help it, can I ?

MRS. RUDGE : You've only got yourself to thank for being copped.

RUDGE : You're not going to start all that again ?

MRS. RUDGE : Why didn't you look round before you started the car ? Too lazy to turn your head.

RUDGE : Oh, for God's sake, Mabel . . .

MRS. RUDGE : I told you not to do that job, but you wouldn't listen to me, oh no, you knew best. Perhaps you'll take a bit of notice next time of what I've got to say. Leaving them all there on the pavement with the furs in their hands and the window smashed and the street full of people . . .

RUDGE : Can't you forget it ?

MRS. RUDGE : No, I can't !

RUDGE: I suppose you *never* made a mistake? Perfect, you are!

MRS. RUDGE: I never done nothing as silly as that.

RUDGE (*getting up*): I've had enough of this. I'm going back to my cell.

MRS. RUDGE: Oh, no, you ain't. Time isn't up yet. We haven't had half an hour yet.

RUDGE: I've had enough. I'd rather be in my cell than sit here listening to you nag, nag, nag!

MRS. RUDGE: That's a nice thing to say to me when I come all this way and spent fifteen and ninepence to cheer you up.

RUDGE: Cheer me up! Christ Almighty! You make me wish I was bloody well dead!

MRS. RUDGE: You ungrateful swine! Spending me precious money to come and 'ear you calling me names.

RUDGE: I ain't calling yer names.

MRS. RUDGE: No. 'Cos yer don't dare. You're afraid. Same as yer was afraid of the bleeding cops.

RUDGE: You shut your trap, or I'll . . .

MORTON: 'Ere! None of that!

MRS. RUDGE: Just you wait till you comes 'ome. I'll tell Freddie about yer.

RUDGE: If I catch that bastard in the 'ouse, I'll wring his neck!

MORTON: 'Ere! Stop it! You know where this will lead to.

RUDGE: Well, tell 'er to leave me alone.

MRS. RUDGE: I'll leave yer alone all right. I'll leave yer flat. Freddie's worth five of you.

RUDGE: Garn! Freddie wouldn't 'ave you at any price.

MRS. RUDGE: Oh, yes 'e would. So would Spike if I gave him 'alf a chance.

RUDGE: Give him a whole chance, then. And bloody good luck to 'im!

MRS. RUDGE: That's right! Turn me into a whore!

RUDGE: Who's turning you into a whore?

MRS. RUDGE: You are, you dirty, rotten pimp!

MORTON (*taking hold of* MRS. RUDGE): Come on now. You've said enough. Out you get!

MRS. RUDGE (*struggling*): You keep your 'ands orf me!

MORTON: If you don't come quiet, I'll blow my whistle.

MRS. RUDGE: All right, blow your whistle. Give 'im one to blow, too. About all he's fit for.

MORTON: Stop your noise, d'you hear? And come along quick.

MRS. RUDGE: Fine burglar, I don't think! Fine bungler, more like! Bungle everything you lay bloody 'ands on!

MORTON *puts his hand over her mouth, and drags her, kicking and struggling, through the door, right. In a few moments he comes back wiping his forehead.*

RUDGE: You know, sir, it's a darn sight more peaceful 'ere in prison, than it is at 'ome listening to 'er blasted nagging tongue. Take me back to me cell!

They go out through the door on the left.

MORTON (*outside*): Take this man back to his work.

MORTON *comes back and goes out through the other door. After a few moments he returns with* LILY PORTER. *She is about seventeen, quite pretty, but with no idea of how to make the best of herself. She wears no make-up and is shabbily dressed. She is nervous and awkward in these strange surroundings.*

MORTON (*indicating a chair*): You sit down there, see? (LILY *obeys him*) Your dad won't be a moment. He'll sit here. You're not to go no nearer to him than that, see?

LILY: Mayn't I . . . Yes, sir.

MORTON: And you're not to give him nothing, see?

LILY: Yes, sir. I haven't brought anything to give him.

MORTON: Some people who ain't used to visiting convicts think they can bring fruit and flowers and all sorts of things, like it was a hospital.

MORTON *goes out.* LILY *looks round at the room, then sits with her eyes on the door.* MORTON *comes back with* PORTER.

PORTER: Why, Lil!

LILY: Hallo, dad.

PORTER: I didn't expect to see you.

MORTON (*to* PORTER): Sit there.

PORTER: Yes, sir. (*He sits opposite* LILY) Where's mum?

LILY: She couldn't come. So . . . so I came.

PORTER: Well, it's lovely to see you, Lil. But I didn't want . . . It's not the place for you.

LILY: Mum thought you'd be disappointed if nobody came. It's been such a long time, now.

PORTER: Why couldn't she come? She's not worse, is she?

LILY: Oh no, dad. It's not that. She said I was

to tell you she's much better. You're not to worry about her, dad.

PORTER : Why couldn't she come, then ?

LILY : She's got a job, and she didn't like to ask them to let her have the day off. She only started Monday, and she didn't want to tell them . . .

PORTER : I see. Of course, she couldn't tell them why she wanted the day off.

LILY : And she didn't want to say she wasn't well or anything, because that might have made them think they'd want to get someone else.

PORTER : What sort of job has she got, Lil ?

LILY : It's in a flat. Awfully easy work, she says. She goes in the morning, and does the rooms out and gets their breakfast, and . . . they're awfully nice to her.

PORTER : But, Lil, she's not well enough for that kind of work.

LILY : Oh, it's awfully easy, really it is, dad. There's only a gentleman and his wife, and just three rooms in the flat. They both go to work. Mum's only there about two hours. And she doesn't have to go at all on Sundays.

PORTER : Well, I suppose it's all right, if she can manage it. You must look after her, Lil. Not let her do too much, will you ?

LILY : No, dad. You mustn't worry. It's all right. Really, it is.

PORTER : She's better, is she ?

LILY : Ever so much better, dad.

PORTER : I'd like to see her. Give her my love, won't you, Lil ? And tell her I'm all right. It's not nearly so bad here as you'd think.

There is a pause.

Thank you for your letters, Lil. It's lovely hearing all the news.

LILY: I'm afraid I'm not much good at writing letters.

PORTER: Course you are, Lil. I love getting them. And you'll be allowed to write more, soon.

LILY: Mum would like to write every day if she could.

PORTER: You might ask her to write in ink, Lil. The pencil's a bit faint, and I like to read them over and over again.

Lily: Yes, dad. I'll tell her.

Another pause.

PORTER: Are you getting on all right at the shop, Lil?

LILY: Yes, dad. I'm not an apprentice any more.

PORTER: Aren't you? What d'you do now?

LILY: I'm assistant to the first hand. I help her with the hats.

PORTER: I expect that's more interesting.

LILY: Oh, yes. I was sick of sewing on buttons and that sort of thing. And I'm getting more money now. Seventeen and six.

PORTER: That's good. How much does mum get?

LILY: A pound.

PORTER: Oh. Well . . . it's not so bad, is it? Not so bad as it was.

LILY: No. It's not so bad as it was.

PORTER: It's all my fault! If I hadn't been such a fool. . . . I've brought disgrace on you, Lil. But I did it for mum. I only did it for her.

LILY: Course you did. You mustn't think about it.

PORTER: I can't help thinking about it. There's nothing else to do here. . . . I wanted to see her get well again, Lil. You mustn't be ashamed of me.

LILY: I'm not, dad. Course I'm not.

PORTER: I was ashamed of myself, at first. But it seems different, now. Being here has made it seem different. Everybody here's done wrong. And there's lots outside have done the same and not got caught. They're decent fellows, most of them. I used to think criminals was different from the rest of us. Some of them are. Couldn't go straight if they tried. But that's only because they've got like that, or they've been brought up wrong. I believe everybody's capable of committing a crime if you put enough temptations in their way. That's why the Lord's Prayer goes like it does: 'Lead us not into temptation.' He knew we wasn't strong enough to resist. If you can keep out of temptation you're all right.

LILY: You mustn't think about all them things, dad. You must think about when you're going to be free again. Won't it be lovely?

PORTER: It's good to see your little face, Lil. That's right—smile. Mum doesn't worry, does she?

LILY: No, dad.

PORTER: I don't want her to worry. When I come out, everything'll be all right. I'll get a job. Some kind of job. I don't suppose it'll be much money, but we'll manage. You must tell her I'll be able to get a job. There's a society that sees to that. Don't forget to tell her that, Lil.

LILY: I won't forget, dad. (*After a pause*) Be nice when we're all together again.

PORTER : I don't think all three of us'll be together for long.

LILY : Why ever not, dad ?

PORTER : You'll be getting married one of these days.

LILY : Oh, go on !

PORTER : Ah, you can talk like that now, but some day. . . . Sure there isn't anybody yet, Lil ? Some nice-looking young fellow ?

LILY : Oh, dad, don't talk so silly !

PORTER : I believe there is !

LILY : There's not !

PORTER : Well, there's plenty of time yet.

A pause.

Perhaps one day we'll be able to have a little house with a garden again.

LILY : Are you still working in the garden here, dad ?

PORTER : Yes. I'm getting quite professional, now. Learning lots about it. I wish you could have seen our tulips this year. Lovely show, we had. D'you remember those pink, double ones we used to have ?

LILY : No, I don't think I do.

PORTER : The pink ones. We only had a few. Out in the front.

LILY : Oh, those. I remember.

PORTER : We had some here. Only a bit deeper pink. They last ever so long.

LILY : Tulips was always your favourites.

PORTER : Oh, I don't know. They're hard to beat.

LILY : I took mum a bunch of tulips when she was in . . . (*stops abruptly.*)

PORTER : What were you going to say, Lil ?

LILY : Nothing . . . I . . . You know, dad . . .

don't you remember, when we both went to see her in hospital? I was thinking of that.

PORTER: That was in the autumn. Chrysanthemums.

LILY: Oh, yes, so they were. How silly of me. I'd forgotten.

PORTER: Lil . . . you're hiding something from me.

LILY: Hiding? Course I'm not. Whatever put that idea in your head?

PORTER: Yes, you are. Lil, what is it?

LILY: Nothing, dad. You old silly!

PORTER: Mum's not in hospital again, is she?

LILY: No. No, dad.

PORTER: You wouldn't tell me an untruth, would you, Lil?

LILY: You know I wouldn't.

PORTER: You're sure she's not in hospital?

LILY: Course I'm sure.

PORTER: Look at me, Lil.

LILY (*looking straight at him; controlling her voice with great difficulty*): Honest, dad. She's not in hospital. I'd tell you if she was.

PORTER: Why did you say that about the tulips?

LILY: (*looking away*) I only made a mistake. I'd forgotten we took chrysanthemums.

PORTER: You're crying, Lil.

LILY: No, I'm not.

PORTER: You are. Why?

LILY: You wouldn't believe what I said.

PORTER: There's something you're keeping back from me. I know there is. You'd better tell me. She isn't . . .

LILY (*crying*): I promised her I wouldn't let you know. She didn't want you to be worried.

PORTER: I thought for a moment she was . . . Don't cry, Lil. It's much better that I should know.

LILY: She was in hospital. We didn't tell you. But it's all right now. Really it is, dad. She's back home now.

PORTER: What happened? Did she have another operation?

LILY: No. Nothing like that.

PORTER: You've got to tell me everything.

LILY: She was awfully ill. She had that pain. And they thought she'd have to have another operation, but when she went into the hospital they decided it wasn't necessary. And so they sent her home.

PORTER: It wasn't necessary. But, Lil, you told me she'd got a job. She couldn't do work like that if she's been ill again.

LILY: She's better now. I told you she was better, dad.

PORTER: You're still not telling me the truth, Lil.

LILY: I am, dad!

PORTER: I know she couldn't be well enough to go out and work. Why didn't she come to-day?

LILY: I've told you.

PORTER: You must tell me the truth, Lil. If you don't tell me everything now, I shan't know what to think.

LILY: She was too ill, dad.

PORTER: I see.

LILY: Oh, dad, she's awful ill! She gets that pain. . . . She won't tell me, but I know she does. . . . I can see. I'm so frightened!

PORTER: No, Lil, you mustn't get frightened.

LILY: The district nurse comes in the evening.

PORTER: Why?

LILY: She gives mum something to make her sleep. Every evening she comes and gives it her. Oh, dad, what's going to happen?

PORTER: Don't cry, Lil. Nothing's going to happen. (*Knowing that what he says is not true*) They wouldn't have sent her home from the hospital if it wasn't all right. They wouldn't have done that if she wasn't getting better.

LILY: She's worse, dad. I know she's worse. Sometimes . . . she's funny . . . she asks for you . . . she doesn't know why you aren't there. . . . Oh, dad, if only you could come home!

PORTER: Yes, if I could see her . . .

LILY: That's what she wants, dad, more than anything. Just to see you.

PORTER: Yes, I must see her . . . Don't cry, Lil. They'll let me come and see her when I tell them she's . . . that she's . . . ill. Don't cry. I'll ask the Governor. He's nice, the Governor; he'll understand.

LILY: D'you think they'll let you, dad? Really?

PORTER: Yes. I'll ask him right away, Lil. Now. There's no time to be lost. I mean . . . the sooner the better. Perhaps they'll let me come to-night, or at any rate to-morrow. You'd better go, Lil, now. We haven't had our half-hour yet, but I'd better see the Governor quick as possible. Now, don't cry, Lil. And you're not to worry, see? Mum will be all right. Good-bye, Lil.

LILY: Good-bye, dad. You will come, won't you?

PORTER: Yes, soon as ever I can. (*To* MORTON) Please, sir, I want to see the Governor.

MORTON: You can't see him now.

PORTER: It's important. We've finished our visit.

MORTON: You haven't had half an hour yet.

PORTER: I know that. But I've got to see the Governor. It's my wife . . .

MORTON: Why don't you finish your visit? It's a long time till the next one.

PORTER: No, it's all right.

MORTON (*going to the door*): Well, it don't make any difference to me. Come on.

PORTER: You will ask the Governor to let me see him . . .

MORTON: Can't be done.

PORTER: Good-bye, Lil. Don't worry. I'll explain to him.

LILY: Good-bye, dad.

PORTER (*as he goes with* MORTON): You see, sir, it's my wife. She's ill. When I tell the Governor he'll let me go and see her . . .

LILY *is still crying.*

CURTAIN

SCENE 4

SCENE: *Outside the cells. All on, as in first scene of the act, except* PORTER. FLEMING *is no longer scrubbing, but sews mail bags with the rest. His eyes are all the time on* BATS, *who never looks up from his work.* BATES *is now reading a novel, which occupies his attention.*

RUDGE: I shan't 'ave the wife 'ere to see me again that's a cert. It don't do.

DUKE: Very wise of you, if I may say so. I've noticed that these visits from relatives often upset a man's nerves.

RUDGE: I don't know nothing about nerves, but my wife can be a proper terror when she likes. Nag yer into the grave, if she got the chance. One thing she 'as done though—made me feel that this place (*looking round*) 'as its advantages. Mrs. Rudge and me is better with a stone wall between us.

DUKE: I gather she was not pleased to see you?

RUDGE: You gather right.

DUKE: Unbalanced creatures, women. Invaluable, when they know their place. But they so seldom do.

BATS (*without looking up*): Let the woman learn in silence with all subjection. But I suffer not a woman to teach, nor to use authority; but to be in silence. For Adam was first formed: then Eve.

RUDGE: Them's my sentiments!

Enter PORTER, *brought back from his visit by* MORTON.

MORTON (*to* PORTER): You can't see the Governor now. How many more times d'you want me to tell you that? Make an application, and you'll see him in the morning. (*To* BATES) One man back, sir.

BATES *changes the number on the slate, then returns to his book.*

PORTER (*almost in tears, to* MORTON): But I've got to

see him at once. It's about my wife. She's ill. Very ill. You don't understand.

MORTON : I understand the rules of this prison all right. And you should do, by this time. Now for God's sake forget it, and finish your work.

PORTER (*making a last attempt*) : Please, sir, ask the Governor if I can see him at once.

MORTON (*wearily*) : It's not my place to ask him. What d'you think he'd say to me if I broke the rules ? I'd get the sack, most likely. You make an application when the officer comes round in the morning—and you'll see the Governor then.

PORTER *sits quietly on his chair*, *but does not take up his work*. *Exit* MORTON.

RUDGE (*sympathetically*) : What's the matter, old cock ? Did you 'ave a lousy visit, too ?

DUKE : Wasn't *your* wife glad to see you ?

PORTER : I didn't see my wife. She's ill. My daughter, Lily, came instead.

RUDGE : Bad luck. Though perhaps if Mrs. Porter 'ad of come, things mightn't of turned out as well as you expected. Me and my old girl 'ad a proper row.

PORTER (*shaking his head*) : My wife and I have never had a row in our lives.

RUDGE : You're a lucky couple.

DUKE : She's ill, you say.

PORTER : Yes. Lil wouldn't tell me at first—didn't want me to know—but I got it out of her in the end. My wife was never strong. But now she's worse. And she wants to see me. I could help her if I saw her. That's what I want to see the Governor about. When I've explained about how ill she is, he may let me go to her.

DUKE : I hate to dash your hopes, but I'm afraid he won't.

PORTER : The Governor's always been very kind to me. Very considerate indeed.

DUKE : Oh, the Governor's all right. A real gentleman. I've always said so. He'd let you go, I've no doubt. But it doesn't rest with him. It's the ones higher up who make the rules.

PORTER : But I *must* see her. They couldn't be so unkind as not to let me just see her. It would make all the difference in the world to us. And it couldn't possibly harm them. Could it ?

Enter SAUNDERS.

SAUNDERS (*to* BATES) : How's the baby, Bates ?

BATES : Fine, sir, thank you.

SAUNDERS : I must look in one afternoon this week and make his acquaintance.

BATES : Thank you, sir. I'm sure my wife would be very pleased.

SAUNDERS : Are any men here coming to Communion to-morrow morning ?

BATS : Please, sir, I'm coming.

SAUNDERS : Yes, Richardson, I've got your name down. Anybody else ?

There is a pause.

PORTER : May I speak to you for a minute, sir ?

SAUNDERS : Of course you may, Porter. What is it ?

PORTER : It's about my wife, sir. She couldn't visit me this afternoon, because she's ill.

SAUNDERS : I'm sorry.

PORTER : Yes, sir. Do you think I might be allowed to go and see her, sir ? Just for a little while. As she can't come and see me ?

SAUNDERS : You mean go to your home ?

PORTER : Just to be with her for a little while, sir. To see each other. I haven't seen her since I came here.

SAUNDERS : I'm afraid that wouldn't be possible, Porter. It has been done, in very extreme cases. But I hope yours isn't a case like that. I mean, your wife's not dying.

PORTER : I don't know . . . she's ill, sir. And seeing me again, just for a few minutes, would make her better. I know it would. Will you see what you can do for me, sir ?

SAUNDERS : You can put your case to the Governor. I'm sure he'll do anything he can for you. But I'm rather afraid that yours is an impossible request. Rules are rules, you know, and all of us have to observe them. You see that, don't you ?

PORTER (*suddenly resigned*) : Yes, sir, I see that. Thank you, sir.

SAUNDERS (*showing paper to* BATES) : Where will I find these two men ? Their cells have been changed, I think.

BATES (*after looking at paper*) : That's right, sir. They're in the other wing. I'll take you to them, sir.

SAUNDERS : Thanks.

BATES (*to* BATS) : Take charge. I'll be back.

BATS : Yes, sir.

BATS *goes to* BATES' *desk. Exit* SAUNDERS *and* BATES.

FLEMING (*to* PORTER) : Cheer up. Your wife will get better. In prison everything seems worse than it really is. One keeps thinking and thinking, because there's nothing else to do. One feels so helpless. One is helpless. But . . .

PORTER (*interrupting; and with a quiet forcefulness that is new to him*): I'm not helpless any longer. She needs me. And I'm going to her.

DUKE: How do you propose to do that?

PORTER (*simply*): I shall escape.

RUDGE: Now don't talk silly.

PORTER (*as one who has a fixed idea*): I shall escape.

FLEMING: Better not try that, old man. It won't get you anywhere.

RUDGE: It'll get you into a punishment cell quick enough. And that's no treat, I can tell you. Bread and water. Loss of remission marks. (*Shaking his head*) Cut out the idea. It ain't worth it.

DUKE (*to* PORTER): They're absolutely right. It's quite impossible to get away from here. Every attempt has failed.

PORTER (*as if he were inspired*): My mind's made up. I *will* escape. I will! (*He looks round at the others defiantly.*)

CURTAIN

END OF ACT II

ACT III

Scene I

SCENE: *Same as Act II, Scene 2.*

The room is empty. The sewing-machine, work-basket, etc., are on the table.

FIELD (*outside*): You go on, Bats. I'll send the Toff up in a few minutes. (*He comes into the room and looks round, then speaks to* FLEMING *who is outside*) Come in here.

FLEMING *comes in. He looks round quickly to see whether* MARY *is in the room.* FIELD *takes a packet of cigarettes out of his pocket and offers one to* FLEMING.

Have a fag?

FLEMING: Thanks. (*He takes one*) Thank you.

FIELD *takes a cigarette himself, and strikes a match.* FLEMING *lights his cigarette from it.*

FIELD: I want to talk to you. (*Lights his own cigarette*). Sit down. FLEMING *sits*. (FIELD *speaks with his back to* FLEMING.) When I married my wife, I knew I was taking a risk. She's younger than me. A lot younger. I thought the risk was worth taking. I had to take it. I was in love with her. Couldn't help myself. (*He turns and faces* FLEMING) I've often wondered what I'd do . . . if . . . if she . . . (*He breaks off and walks across the room. Again he speaks with his back to* FLEMING) You see, I didn't marry her because I wanted a wife. Not just someone to cook and look after things. I was used to living alone. I didn't mind it. She didn't feel the same way about me as I did about her. I knew that. But I thought we'd get along together all right. I thought she might get fond of me in a way. And she did. (*Faces* FLEMING) I know she did. I can't tell you how much that meant to me. But, of course, she didn't really love me. Not in the way I love her. I couldn't expect that. Though I . . . I always hoped for it. Bloody silly of me, wasn't it ?

FLEMING : Why are you telling me all this ?

FIELD : We've got to know where we stand. Haven't we ?

FLEMING : I don't know what you mean.

FIELD : When Bats came into this room yesterday afternoon, he found you both together.

FLEMING : You said I could come down and have something to eat.

FIELD : He told me she had her arms round you. You were sitting over there.

FLEMING : He's crazy. You know he's crazy.

FIELD : Not in that way. He don't invent things.

FLEMING : You can't mean you believe him ?

FIELD : He was telling the truth. He always does. I couldn't believe it at first. You see, I didn't want to. I was going to ask her myself. That seemed the best way. But I didn't have to. I could see. She's been different lately. Nothing very much, but . . . little things.

FLEMING : I tell you, it's not true. Oh yes, she did have her arms round me . . . I was . . . You don't know what it's like. I was telling her . . . I had to talk to someone . . . she was only trying to comfort me. There was nothing more in it than that.

FIELD: Then why has she been different to me lately?

FLEMING: You've imagined it.

FIELD: Oh, no, I haven't imagined anything. You've got to tell me the truth.

FLEMING: I've told you.

FIELD: No, you haven't. It's no good lying about it. That won't make it better for any of us. It only makes it worse. We've got to get this all straight.

FLEMING: If you won't believe me, ask her. Why don't you ask her?

FIELD: I daren't. What am I to do if she says she loves you? What am I to do then?

FLEMING: She won't tell you that.

FIELD: This is my only chance, talking to you. You and I might get things straightened out. If we drag her into it, that'll finish it. If only you'd tell me the truth!

FLEMING: I have told you.

FIELD: You needn't be afraid I'll try and get my own back on you. I swear to you, I won't do anything, to you or her. But I've got to know.

FLEMING: You won't believe me until I tell you a lie.

FIELD: It's not your fault if she loves you. It's not her fault either. I've got to know whether you love her. Then I can tell what to do. I don't know where I am now.

FLEMING: But I tell you . . . Oh, what's the use? You won't believe me.

FIELD: If she doesn't love you, why did she have her arms round you?

FLEMING : I'd been crying, that's why. She felt sorry for me.

FIELD : You had your head on her breast.

FLEMING : No !

FIELD : She had her arms round you.

FLEMING : Oh, for God's sake, stop ! I can't stand it any longer.

FIELD : I could fix it so as you'd never see her again. You've got another three and a half years here. Yesterday she started asking me questions about how long it takes for a man to go crazy when he's inside. I wondered why she was so worked up about it. Yes . . . I could fix it so as you didn't see each other. And then I'd tell her you'd gone mad.

FLEMING : You can't do that !

FIELD : What's to prevent me ?

FLEMING : You'd kill her if you told her that. She loves me.

There is silence for a few seconds.

FIELD (*in a flat voice*) : She loves you. Yes. I've got to get used to that.

FLEMING : God, how I wish this had never happened !

FIELD : Why ? Why d'you wish that ?

FLEMING : You've been so decent to me. I feel such a swine !

FIELD : You said that she loves you. You didn't say whether you love her. Do you ?

FLEMING : Yes . . . yes. I think I do. I don't know.

FIELD : You think you do ! Have you told her that you *think* you love her ? I suppose you've made some sort of plans. Does she mean to go away with you when you're released ?

FLEMING : Yes.

FIELD : I see. She's going to live with me for over three years—and sleep with me—and then go away with you. I wouldn't want a woman I loved to do a thing like that.

FLEMING : We couldn't think of anything else.

FIELD : What are you going to do afterwards? She's not your class.

FLEMING : After this, I don't think it's going to matter much what class I belong to.

FIELD : How are you going to keep her?

FLEMING : We haven't thought about all that.

FIELD : Have you thought about anything? How are you going to live?

FLEMING : I don't know.

FIELD : Your class is about the only thing you will have when you leave this place. You're a gentleman. That'll be your one hope.

FLEMING : I'll get along somehow.

FIELD : You haven't got much to offer her, have you?

FLEMING : We love each other.

FIELD : She loves you. You've been inside for eighteen months. Until you came over to do this job you hadn't seen a woman all that time. And she's a good-looking girl. She was sorry for you, and kind to you, wasn't she? Spoke to you in a way you weren't used to. Any woman with a soft heart would have done the same. But she fell in love with you. Would you have looked twice at her if you'd seen her before you came here?

FLEMING : I don't know. I don't know anything now! I can't think . . .

FIELD : You can't do things like this without knowing what you're about.

FLEMING : You don't know what it's like . . . day after day . . .

FIELD : You've learnt to pity yourself, haven't you ?

FLEMING : We all do that.

FIELD : It's the beginning of the rot.

FLEMING : What ?

FIELD : You start feeling sorry for yourself, and then your self-respect goes.

FLEMING : Self-respect ! I've forgotten when I had that. I've forgotten everything that's normal and decent.

FIELD : There's one decent thing you can do now. You've got to tell her you don't love her.

FLEMING : I can't. Why d'you want me to ? You can do what you like. You've got me where you want me.

FIELD : I could make your life hell if I wanted to. That wouldn't help me. I've always felt sorry for you. You made a mess of things, and they sent you here. You'll never get back. You may get another chance, if you're damned lucky. But you'll never escape from this place. Things happen to you here that make you different. You'll have to fight, but you'll have to fight alone. You can't ask anyone else to share your life. You're not the kind of man that can live on a woman's love. You couldn't keep it up. You'd go rotten.

FLEMING : Yes. . . . It was only a dream. The real thing is too horrible to think about. And so you start imagining things. Perhaps that's how people start to go mad.

FIELD : You're going to tell her, aren't you ?

FLEMING: I can't. I'd better not see her again.

FIELD: You must tell her.

FLEMING: I can write.

FIELD: No. She's got to hear you say it. She'll only believe it if you tell her yourself.

FLEMING: I'll tell her.

FIELD (*looking out of the window*): Try and make it easy for her. As easy as you can. I don't suppose she's felt like this about anyone before. But she'll forget. Perhaps she'll be fond of me again, one day.

FLEMING: I mustn't see her after this. You'll make sure of that, won't you?

FIELD: Yes. Here she comes, now. She's been shopping in the town. She's hurrying. She must know you're here. (*Turns away from the window*) I'll ask her to get you something to eat, like I always do. She must never guess that I know . . .

FLEMING: All right.

FIELD: Go up on the roof when you've spoken to her. Then I'll know when to come back.

FIELD *goes out.* FLEMING *is alone for a few moments.* MARY *comes in wearing a hat and coat. She takes off the hat as she goes to* FLEMING.

MARY: He's gone out. We've got a little while together. (*Puts her arms round* FLEMING. *He holds her in his arms and kisses her mechanically*) My dear . . . (*holds him close to her so that she does not see his face*) You're so early to-day. Much earlier than usual. I saw Bats on the roof as I was coming along. I wanted to run, but I didn't dare. We've got to be so careful. Let me get this coat off. (*As she is taking off her coat she sees his face. He is staring at her fixedly*) What's the matter? Why are you looking at me like that?

FLEMING: What?

MARY: Are you going to finish that job to-day?

FLEMING: Yes.

MARY: You won't be coming here any more.

FLEMING: No. We'll finish it to-day. We shan't be coming here any more. I shan't see you . . .

MARY: I'm not going to cry. I don't want you to see me with my nose all red. . . . It always does go bright red when I cry! (*Puts her arms round him again and her head on his breast*) It'll be all right, darling. We'll see each other sometimes. I'll think of some way of getting you here to do another job.

FLEMING: I don't want you to do that.

MARY: But it's the only way. I'll be very careful. He'll never guess.

FLEMING: I'm not going to see you again.

MARY: Yes, darling, you will. I promise you I'll manage something.

FLEMING (*holding her away from him by the shoulders*): We're not going to see each other again. Never.

MARY (*frightened*): Don't . . .

FLEMING: We've got to forget all about this. It hasn't really meant anything. It's been a dream. We'll forget it when we wake up.

MARY: What's the matter? Darling . . . darling . . . what . . .

FLEMING: It all seemed right. Things do seem right in dreams. Fantastic, impossible things. But all the time you know it's not really true. You don't want to wake up. But you have to.

MARY: You don't know what you're saying. Derek, my darling, don't look at me like that!

MARY (*acting*) : Oh ! You gave me quite a start. I didn't hear you.

FIELD (*after a pause*) : Soon be finished, won't it ?

MARY : There's quite a lot to do yet.

FIELD : It's a pretty colour. It'll suit you.

MARY : Think so ?

FIELD (*puts his hand on her shoulder*) : Yes. You'll look very pretty in that. You look pretty in anything.

MARY (*pats his hand*) : Silly boy !

CURTAIN

SCENE 2

SCENE : *A punishment cell. This is like any other cell, only with all furniture removed except a low stool. A Bible is on the shelf fixed in the wall.*

When the curtain rises PORTER *is sitting on the stool, in the corner farthest from the door. His face is buried in his hands and he is quite motionless.*

The door is unlocked by an officer to admit BATS, *who enters carrying a bucket of water and a scrubbing brush.*

BATS : Here's a bucket and brush for you to clean out your cell with. (*As there is no answer, or movement*) I said, here's a bucket and brush for you to clean out your cell.

Slowly PORTER *raises his head. There is a vacant look in his eyes.*

Did you hear what I said?

PORTER *nods his head.*

You haven't lost your tongue, have you?

PORTER: A little while ago I was talking to myself. It frightened me. They say that men who are going mad begin by doing that.

BATS: They say a lot of things here, and not a word of truth in any of them. I talk to myself, often. But I'm not mad, am I?

PORTER (*hesitatingly*): No. No, you're not mad.

BATS: Then there's no need to be worrying yourself.

PORTER: Shut up here alone, with nothing to do for hours on end—(*covering his face with his hands again*) It's terrible . . .

BATS: Every sin brings its own punishment. You should have stopped to consider, before trying to escape. It wasn't right to do that, you know.

PORTER: I wanted to see my wife. She's very ill.

BATS: There's men here wants all sorts of things, but they can't have them. You ought to know that. How much longer are you to be here?

PORTER: Another two days. (*Desperately*) I don't think I can stand it. I'm starved, too. They only give me bread and water.

BATS: A man can stand a lot when it comes to the test. You'll be all right.

PORTER: With nothing to do, the time goes so slowly. Every hour seems like a whole day.

BATS (*pointing*): There's your Bible. You can read that. There's more than enough reading in that book to last a man a lifetime.

PORTER: I don't find it very interesting.

BATS (*exasperated*): The Bible not interesting, did you say? Who may you be to judge the greatest book in the world? Answer me that.

PORTER: Please don't be angry with me.

BATS: I'm not angry with you—just full of pity for your ignorance. A man can read the Bible every day of his life, and still be learning at the end. (*More kindly*) There's much in that book you'll find helpful. Often men turn to it in their trouble—and are saved.

PORTER (*taking Bible from shelf*): I will read it.

BATS: That's right. (*He goes towards the door, and as he does so the prison band starts playing outside*) There's the band to cheer you up. For once they're playing a more decent tune.

SAUNDERS *enters. He looks grave.*

Good evening, sir.

SAUNDERS: Good evening, Richardson.

Exit BATS. SAUNDERS *stands staring at* PORTER, *unable to begin. The sound of the band dies away.*

PORTER (*getting to his feet*): Is something the matter, sir?

SAUNDERS: I'm afraid so, Porter. You must be brave. Very brave. I've got—bad news for you.

PORTER (*alarmed*): Not more punishment! I couldn't bear it, sir. Really, I couldn't.

SAUNDERS: No, you won't be punished any more.

PORTER: I'm so hungry. So cold. They couldn't treat an animal worse.

SAUNDERS: It's wrong that you, or anybody else, should be treated so inhumanly. I ought not to have said that. But it's what I feel.

PORTER: What is it, sir?

SAUNDERS: You must be brave. Very brave. It's your wife. *The two men stare at each other.*

PORTER (*so quietly*): My wife's dead. That's what you've come to tell me, isn't it?

SAUNDERS *nods; then catches hold of* PORTER, *who sways unsteadily. Then* PORTER *stands apart, dazed.*

(*Slowly*) They've killed her. That's what they've done. Killed her.

SAUNDERS: You must believe that we didn't know how serious . . .

PORTER (*interrupting, and with gentle authority*): Not you. Nor the Governor. You couldn't help it.

SAUNDERS (*putting an arm round his shoulder*): Shall we pray together? It might help.

Together they kneel.

Our Father, which art in Heaven, hallowed be Thy name . . .

PORTER: Our Father, which art in Heaven, hallowed be Thy name . . .

SAUNDERS: Thy Kingdom come, Thy will be done on earth, as it is in Heaven . . .

PORTER: Thy Kingdom come, Thy will be done on earth, as it is in Heaven . . .

SAUNDERS: Give us this day our daily bread, and forgive us our trespasses, as we forgive them that trespass against us . . .

PORTER (*after a pause, and in a slightly changed voice*): . . . as we forgive them that trespass against us . . . (*He starts to sob.*)

SAUNDERS (*against the sobbing*): Lead us not into temptation, but deliver us from evil. For Thine is the Kingdom, the Power and the Glory, for ever and ever. —Amen.

SAUNDERS *rises to his feet, but* PORTER *remains kneeling, his eyes closed.*

(*Looking down at him*) I'll get an officer to bring your bed in. You'll feel better lying down.

SAUNDERS *goes out.* *When* PORTER *opens his eyes, he sees the bucket of water.* *He ties his handkerchief over his mouth and drags the bucket towards him. He puts his head into the bucket of water.* *At the same time* MORTON *arrives with the bed-board, which he drops, rushing forward.*

MORTON: Here! What are you doing! You bloody fool!

MORTON *struggles with* PORTER, *and at the same time manages to blow his whistle.* FIELD *arrives, sees what is happening, and helps to control* PORTER, *who is struggling madly.* BATES *arrives.*

FIELD (*to* BATES): Get the strait-jacket!

For a minute PORTER *ceases to struggle, remaining limp in the grasp of the two officers.*

Trying to drown yourself. Haven't you more sense?

MORTON: If I hadn't of come in when I did, he'd have done himself in.

The band outside plays "Land of Hope and Glory."

PORTER *starts to struggle again.* BATES *enters with strait-jacket.* *With some difficulty the officers manage to strap* PORTER *into it.* *They leave him, on the floor in the middle of the cell.*

FIELD (*who is the last of the officers to exit, turns at the door, before closing it*): I'm sorry, Porter. (*He closes door.*)

PORTER *groans.* *The music swells as the light fades.*

CURTAIN

Scene 3

SCENE : *The Governor's office : three and a half years later. When the curtain rises the* GOVERNOR *is seated at his desk, writing letters.* BATES *enters carrying the evening paper.*

GOVERNOR (*looking up*) : What is it, Bates ?

BATES : Your evening paper, sir.

GOVERNOR : Oh, thanks.

BATES (*putting paper on desk*) : There's something in it, sir, about a man who was here. Richardson. Bats, we used to call him. Been gone a year now.

GOVERNOR : Old 'Bats' Richardson ? What's he been up to ?

BATES : It seems he's gone mad, sir. He always did strike me as being a bit queer in the head. Religious, you know.

GOVERNOR (*smiling*) : Is religion always a sign of madness ?

BATES : I didn't mean that, sir. Only Richardson was always preaching at the other men. Funny, he was. He thinks he's God now. It says so there.

GOVERNOR (*who has been reading paper, puts it down*) : Poor old chap. (*Reflectively*) Fifteen years in prison, and at the end of it—certified insane. (*Looking at* BATES) Rather terrible, isn't it ?

BATES : I don't think he really wanted to leave here, sir. You can understand it in a way. Nobody outside has got much use for them.

GOVERNOR (*more to himself*): Nobody. Unwanted. Forgotten.

House-telephone rings.

Yes? Oh, that you, Saunders. Certainly. No. I'll come along now. Right. (*Puts down the receiver. To* BATES) I'm going along to the chaplain's office. I've asked a couple of men who are going out to-morrow to come and see me. (*Looks at note-book*) Fleming and Porter. Tell them . . .

There is a knock at the door.

Come in!

MORTON *enters, with* FLEMING.

Ah, here's one of them. All right, Morton. (MORTON *salutes, and goes out. To* FLEMING) I shan't be a few minutes. Wait for me here, will you?

FLEMING: Thank you, sir.

Exit GOVERNOR, *leaving* FLEMING *and* BATES. *The subtle change which imprisonment has made in* FLEMING *shows itself in his cynical manner. We did not notice this in the earlier scenes.*

BATES: So you're leaving us to-morrow?

FLEMING: At eight o'clock in the morning. In a suit of clothes that I haven't worn for nearly five years. I wonder how it will fit me.

BATES: You'll be too bucked to care. Is somebody coming to meet you at the gate?

FLEMING: I should think it's highly improbable.

BATES: Decided what you're going to do? In the way of a job, I mean?

FLEMING: I'm thinking of trading the only asset I've got.

BATES: And what's that?

FLEMING: Well, I believe I have the appearance of what is called—a gentleman.

BATES: Will that be much use?

FLEMING (*with meaning*): Most useful—in gaining people's confidence.

BATES: Confidence trick, eh? But that's criminal.

FLEMING: I am a criminal.

BATES: Oh, but you're different.

FLEMING: Thank you—sir. But I doubt if anybody outside will appreciate the difference.

BATES: Well, I'm sorry you're going.

FLEMING: I'm not.

BATES: I bet you aren't. I had a letter from Mr. Field the other day. He asked how you was getting on.

FLEMING (*interested*): Field. Nice chap. Always very decent to me. Didn't he get transferred to a prison in the north somewhere?

BATES: That's right. I was sorry, too, when he went.

FLEMING (*after a pause*): Did you ever hear why he asked to be transferred?

BATES: On account of his wife, I think.

FLEMING: Really?

Enter the GOVERNOR.

GOVERNOR: Ah, there you are, Fleming. All right, Bates.

Exit BATES.

I thought I'd like a little chat with you before you leave us. Sit down, Fleming.

FLEMING: Thank you, sir. (*He sits down.*)

GOVERNOR (*sitting at his desk*): Have you any plans for the future?

FLEMING: None that I care to discuss.

GOVERNOR (*regarding him steadily*): I see. (*A pause*) I merely asked because I understand that you told the Discharged Prisoners Aid Society that you had no need of their services. From that I hoped that you had relatives or friends to go to.

FLEMING: I've got no relatives. And I doubt if I shall find any friends left.

GOVERNOR: That's a rather gloomy view to take, isn't it?

FLEMING: It seems to me the only sane one.

GOVERNOR: Too many men, you know, get the idea that because they've been in prison, they're finished. Done for . . .

FLEMING: Aren't they?

GOVERNOR (*rather too glibly*): Not at all. There are many men in the world to-day who have put their imprisonment behind them. Forgotten it. Men who are now respected citizens. They've paid their debt to society, and started a new life . . .

FLEMING: Do you think, sir, that one ever really starts a new life? (*Shaking his head*) I don't. Any more than I think that society accepts the debt that a man pays with his imprisonment. A prisoner goes on being punished—always. I've heard, and seen enough while I've been here, to know that that's the truth.

GOVERNOR (*uneasily*): You mustn't think that, Fleming.

FLEMING: What alternative have I? (*Bitterly*) I did wrong. I was found out. And to be found out is the unforgivable sin. After that one's very presence is an embarrassment, to others. All that's left for men in my position is to bury themselves. All the comfort they're ever likely to find must be amongst men like themselves. Other convicts.

GOVERNOR: It hurts me to hear you talk like that.

FLEMING: I believe you, sir. It hurts you because, being a sensible man, you know it's true.

GOVERNOR: I'm not sure that it is.

FLEMING: You don't want to be sure. But in your heart you are. Can you forget, for a moment, our relative positions; and answer me a very plain question?

GOVERNOR: Certainly.

FLEMING: Will you, after my release to-morrow, ask me to dine with you and your family? (*There is a long pause*) You'd like to perhaps, but you dare not. It wouldn't be *right*. An ex-convict has his place in the world—that of an ex-convict.

There is another pause.

GOVERNOR: I'm afraid you can find no redeeming features in our prison system.

FLEMING: In your system—no. But once, someone . . .

GOVERNOR: I don't think I'd better ask you about that.

FLEMING: It was momentary. But while it lasted, I felt a man again. In prison that's a rare, and very wonderful feeling.

GOVERNOR (*rising*): I think I understand. (*Holds out his hand*) Good-bye, Fleming. Good luck.

FLEMING (*taking his hand*): Good-bye, sir. And thank you for your kindness to me. I'll always remember that.

FLEMING *goes out.* GOVERNOR *speaks into house-telephone.*

GOVERNOR: Send in Porter, will you? Thanks.

There is a knock at the door.

Come in.

Enter BATES.

BATES: Excuse me, sir, three four five five, Rudge, would like to see you for a moment.

GOVERNOR: Rudge wants to see me, does he? Send him in.

BATES: Yes, sir. (*Speaking through the door*) This way.

Enter RUDGE. *Exit* BATES.

GOVERNOR: Well, Rudge, what is it? I didn't send for you because, in your case, I thought any parting advice would be useless. What's the trouble?

RUDGE: No trouble, sir.

GOVERNOR: Well, what is it?

RUDGE: I wonder, sir, if you could see your way to doing me a small favour?

GOVERNOR: A favour? Bit late, isn't it? To-morrow, at eight thirty, you'll have your freedom.

RUDGE: That's just it, sir. I wondered if you'd mind letting me have an early release, say . . . seven-thirty. It would make a great difference to me.

GOVERNOR: I see no objection. Have you any special reason for the request?

RUDGE: It's like this, sir . . . in her last letter, my wife said she'd be waiting outside the gate for me at eight-thirty, sharp.

GOVERNOR: But if you leave an hour earlier you'll miss your wife.

RUDGE: That is the idea, sir. Last time she came here we had an awful row. Don't want her to start it all over again outside the gate. Might get the place a bad name.

GOVERNOR (*amused*): I see. Naturally, you want to avoid that.

RUDGE: If I can, sir.

GOVERNOR: Very well, Rudge. I'll see that your name is put down for an early release to-morrow.

RUDGE: Thank you very much, sir.

GOVERNOR: I suppose there's no chance of you giving up burglary? I suppose you're going out to be a bigger and better burglar?

RUDGE: That's my ambition.

GOVERNOR: Ah, well, I suppose I'll be seeing you again one of these days.

RUDGE: If I ever do have the bad luck to come inside again, I hope I'll find you here. In charge! Good-bye, sir, and good luck.

GOVERNOR: Good-bye, Rudge. Oh, you'll find Porter outside; send him in, will you?

RUDGE: A pleasure, sir. (*He goes out.*)

PORTER *comes into the room and stands not far from the door. His expression these days can best be described as wooden, and his voice disinterested, when it is not bitter.*

Come in, Porter. Sit down.

PORTER *does as he is told.*

So, you're leaving us, Porter?

PORTER: Yes, sir.

GOVERNOR: And do you know what you are going to do with your future?

PORTER: My future's not worth much.

GOVERNOR: I know that your plans are really no business of mine. But if you think it might help to speak of them, and I can give you any advice . . .

PORTER (*quickly*): You can't give me any advice. (*More considerately*) Thank you, all the same, sir.

GOVERNOR (*trying to draw him*): I expect you'll be making your home with your daughter now?

PORTER: My daughter's married now—to a good man.

GOVERNOR: And you don't think of living with them for a while? Until you're more settled.

PORTER: And spoil my daughter's happiness?

GOVERNOR: What is your son-in-law's attitude?

PORTER: He doesn't know about me. And he'll never know. I've told my girl that. Perhaps we'll meet sometimes—secretly.

GOVERNOR: But have you any means, Porter?

PORTER: A man who's in here with me is going to look after me.

GOVERNOR: It's not always wise, Porter, to associate outside with men one's met in here. They don't always make the best companions.

PORTER: This man has been kind to me. I've learned to be grateful for kindness. I've nothing against anybody here. They're not free to do as they'd like. Are they, sir?

GOVERNOR: Perhaps not, Porter. We're all responsible to a higher authority.

PORTER: The men who make the laws. And the judges who enforce them. It would do them good to come to a prison, to see for themselves. But they're too busy, of course. They might not like what they saw, either. So it's better for them not to look too closely. I've reasoned it all out, sitting in my cell.

GOVERNOR (*seeing there is no point to be gained*): I'm sorry there is nothing I can do for you. (*As* PORTER *reaches the door*) You wouldn't like me to write to your daughter for you? (PORTER *shakes his head*) Very well, Porter.

PORTER *goes out. Left alone, the* GOVERNOR *sits down again and rests his head in his hands. The door opens, and* SAUNDERS *comes in.*

SAUNDERS: Are you coming to have a look at the Receptions, sir? There are several new men in to-night. Long sentences, too—as you'll see from your list.

GOVERNOR (*as he crosses the room to the door*): I'd rather interview the men coming into this prison than those going out of it. They're like children when they come in—most of them. But they end up—tough problems.

CURTAIN